The *storms of life* will threaten to *rock your world*. But your *personal forecast* of God's Word will bring hope, healing, faith, love, peace, and victory through Christ Jesus.

Table of Contents

Introduction ix
God's Word is Supernatural 1
    Lesson 1. Jesus's Teaching Ministry 3
Study, Meditate, Believe, and Speak God's Word 13
    Lesson 2. God's Will is Healing 15
    Lesson 3. Natural Knowledge vs. Revelation Knowledge . 25
    Lesson 4. Healing Belongs to You 37
Believe God and Act in Agreement with His Word 45
    Lesson 5. Receive Communion 47
    Lesson 6. By the Stripes of Jesus 55
    Lesson 7. Enter into Rest 61
    Lesson 8. Activate God's Power 69
Let the Word Dominate Your Thoughts, Emotions, and Actions . 75
    Lesson 9. Take Authority Over All Thoughts 77
    Lesson 10. God Sent His Word to Heal 83
To receive healing, you must make the truth of
healing more real than the symptoms in your body 89
    Lesson 11. Take Hold of Your Healing 91

Lesson 12. God's Word is Power-Packed 101

Lesson 13. God's Healing Power. 111

Five Minutes a Day in the Word is not going to Counterbalance Sixteen Hours of Unbelief. 119

Lesson 14. God's Healing Scriptures. 121

Healing Is Warfare. It's Not a Reward for Being Good 133

Appendices 135

Final Words. 137

Satan Steals from Us 139

What About Medical Science? 141

Guidelines to Use to Interpret Scripture. 143

Introduction

You can plant spiritual seeds that will produce physical healing! How? According to God's instructions, you can produce healing by speaking and declaring what God's Word promises about it. The same is true for freedom from fear, addiction, anxiety, emotional stress, depression, and disease.

In the beginning, God the Creator established that *everything* would reproduce as a seed (plants, trees, vegetables, animals, people). The seed of God's Word, sown in your heart, also produces "after its own kind" (**Gen. 1:11; Mark 4:26-28**).

Most people only consider facts that relate to the physical senses (feel, taste, hear, see, and smell), but there is a wonderful unseen kingdom that God wants to open to us that will reveal the secrets of life. God's powerful words are *seeds* that will help you conquer sickness, addictions, fear, worry, doubt, and disease. God's words are supernatural!

God, the Creator of everything, is a spirit (**John 4:24**). God's words are spirit and life (**John 6:63**). God is upholding all things by the word of His power (**Heb. 1:3**). It may not seem right to our natural thinking, but God's *words* are the *seeds of our miracle* (**Mark 4:13-20**).

How do we activate a seed to produce? The way we plant the seed of anything is the same way God did in the beginning. He believed and He "spoke" (God planted His Word to create the earth.) We activate a seed of healing, prosperity, or freedom from fear by speaking and declaring God's Word aloud.

Excellent Health Was Interrupted

From October 2021 to January 2022, I was attacked with a barrage of sickness and disease. During those 4 months, the enemy attacked me with kidney pain, a urethral stone, a prostate problem, an inguinal hernia, a stroke, covid, and a threatening tumor.

While in the hospital for the stroke, a MRI/cat scan discovered that the large tumor was almost certain to be malignant.

In one sense I knew that I was in a fight. I needed to build my faith in God and His Word, resist the devil, and drain the doubt. On the other hand, my senses and body were screaming with pain that I could not deny. I found myself in a position that it was extremely hard to "walk by faith, not by sight." (**2 Cor. 5:7**)

Previous to the stroke, in another examination – the doctor discovered that I had an inguinal hernia, high blood pressure, and suggested that I also needed a resection of the prostate.

During one of the operations, the surgeon discovered that I had a large 2 cm urethral stone, which explained why I also had severe pain. Now, before you think these problems were just normal – while fixing the hernia, the doctor confirmed that I had a large stage 3 tumor that must come out immediately. It was demonic oppression.

I'm giving all these details only to give you hope and encouragement that you too can use God's way to overcome all attacks to your health. What is God's way? Believe and speak the Word!

You might not agree, but in my opinion, this was an evil spiritual attack from the enemy. I know this for sure; God did <u>not</u> do this to me. God is love and God is good. The devil is the one who steals, kills, and destroys (**John 10:10**).

I had a lot of time to examine my faith in the love of God during my healing journey. I now have a renewed appreciation for the power of God's Words to heal (**Psalm 107:20**). I wish I would have had a better *revelation* of God's Word being the seed to plant in my heart – and draining the doubt and unbelief that the world system promotes – before I had to go through my healing journey!

During the operations that I went through, my wife began to lead us in communion every day. She also started speaking to the 3-stage tumor to wither and die at the root. And it was blackened and withered!

I believe with all my heart that my wife, Pam, had revelation knowledge to speak like Jesus did against the unfruitful fig tree (**Mark 11:20-22**).

Are you trying to believe God for healing? Have you been speaking the Scriptures, meditating on them, and planting them in your heart? If you haven't, then you are probably wondering why you aren't seeing any results.

In the natural realm, you cannot grow anything without a seed. It's the same way in the spiritual realm; everything comes from the seed of God's Word planted in your heart. This law of seedtime and harvest operates in every area of our lives. If we plant God's Word in our hearts, then allow the seed to germinate and the plant to grow to maturity, we will reap the fruit of a harvest. That is God's best!

Yes, a person can get healed without planting God's Word in his or her heart. It comes through the prayers of others with the gifts of healing (**1 Cor. 12:9**), but it is not God's best. We should never be too proud to ask for help, but the proper way to get healed is to take God's promises of healing and plant them in our hearts until they release their life-giving power into our physical bodies.

Here are four powerful gifts that the Lord has *already* given to us to receive His blessing and healing.

1. By the stripes of Jesus, we are already healed. (**1 Peter 2:24**) Jesus bore our sicknesses at the same time He bore our sins. It's a done deal in the spirit realm. That's why we need to speak to the problem, (**Mark 11:23**), and pray "Your will be done on earth as it is in heaven. (**Matt. 6:9-10**.)

2. Sowing and reaping. God's Word is the seed to plant in our hearts. The harvest is the supernatural fruit of healing and blessing! (**Mark 4; Gen. 1**)

3. The gifts of the Spirit (**1 Cor. 12-14; Rom. 12:3-9**)

4. The believer's authority (**Matt. 16:18-19; Mark 16:17-18; Luke 10:19**)

God's Word is Supernatural

Lesson 1

Jesus's Teaching Ministry

The sower sows the word.
And these are the ones by the wayside where the word is sown.
When they hear, Satan comes immediately and takes away the word
that was sown in their hearts.

Mark 4:14-15

In Mark 4, the Lord taught several parables which illustrate that the Word of God is to the kingdom of God what a natural seed is to a harvest. The first of these parables, the story of the sower, is the key to unlocking all of the Word of God (**Mark 4:13**). If we don't understand these truths, Jesus said we won't understand any of His other parables.

There are many life-changing truths in these parables, but one fact must be understood to get the full benefit of this teaching. The Lord used the comparison of His Word to a law of nature that is unchangeable, and that is that God's spiritual laws work the same as gravity and electricity.

Here's what I mean. You can manipulate nearly all systems that men have created. The legal system can be beaten, letting the guilty go free. Our educational system can be beaten, passing students who haven't really learned the material. But you *can't* change the law of seedtime and harvest.

What if a farmer waited until he saw his neighbors reaping their crops before he sowed for his crop? Regardless of how sincere he was or the justification for not sowing his seed at the proper time, he would not reap a crop overnight. *The law of seedtime and harvest cannot be violated.*

This is why our Lord chose to compare the way His Word works to a seed. There is a germination process of the Word of God in your life that takes time and can't be avoided. In the second parable of **Mark 4:26-29,** Jesus said,

> *"So is the kingdom of God, as if a man should cast seed into the ground; And should sleep, and rise night and day, and the seed should spring and grow up, he knoweth not how. For the earth bringeth forth fruit of herself; first the blade, then the ear, after that the full corn in the ear. But when the fruit is brought forth, immediately he putteth in the sickle, because the harvest is come."*

The seed is the Word of God (verse 14) and the ground is our hearts (verse 15). Our hearts were created by God to bring forth fruit when

His Word is planted in them. Just as a seed must remain in the ground over time to germinate, so the Word of God has to abide in us.

> Jesus said in **John 15:7**, *"If ye abide in me, and my words abide in you, ye shall ask what ye will, and it shall be done unto you."*

What would happen if you planted a seed in your garden and then dug it up each morning to see if anything was happening? It would die and never produce fruit. You have to have faith that the seed is doing what God created it to do.

Some people put God's Word in their hearts for a day or two, but if they don't see fruit almost immediately, they dig up the seed through their negative words and actions and wonder why it doesn't work. You have to leave it in the ground over time. Then, there are also different stages of growth.

> **Mark 4:28** says, *"First the blade, then the ear, after that the full corn in the ear."*

Many people are impatient, wanting to bypass the growth cycle and get the full ear right now. I've actually had to tell people that what they were believing God for was not going to happen, not because the vision wasn't good, but because they were expecting a complete ear of corn immediately.

God's Spiritual Laws

God's kingdom operates on laws, like the laws that govern the fruit-bearing process of a seed. God will not give you the full ear of corn if you haven't seen the first blade. That's the way God's kingdom works, and this is precisely the reason most people don't see God's best come to pass in their lives. They think that since God loves them, He will just grant their request regardless of whether they put the miracle of the seed to work or not.

Look at what happened after Jesus taught His disciples these principles of the seed.

> **Mark 4:35** says, *"On the same day, when evening had come, He said to them, 'Let us cross over to the other side.'"*

In a sense, Jesus was giving them a test. On the same day that He taught them the principles of God's Word as a seed, He gave them a seed. He said, *"Let us cross over to the other side."* He didn't say, "Let us go halfway across and drown." The disciples had a seed from the lips of the Creator that gave them authority over the creation.

What happened? A two-hour trip turned into a fight for the disciples' lives. Instead of using the seed the Lord had given them, they did all they knew to do in the natural and then were disappointed with the Lord.

They said in verse 38, *"Teacher, do You not care that we are perishing?"*

This wasn't a cabin cruiser. Jesus was in an open boat full of water (verse 37) sloshing all around Him. He was well aware of their plight and yet was trying to sleep. They wanted Him to pick up a bucket and bail, row, or do something.

How did Jesus respond? Did He apologize and say, "I'm sorry, guys. I was really tired?" No!

Instead, He said, *"Why are you so fearful? How is it that you have no faith?"* (Verse 40). Jesus was telling them that they should have stilled the storm. If they would have operated in faith instead of fear, that's exactly what they could have done.

God Has Done His Part

The Lord did His job by giving them the seed of His Word. Their job was to take the seed and make it work. Instead, they doubted Jesus's love for them and thought He didn't care. Likewise, we often complain to the Lord, "Don't You love me? Why aren't You healing me or prospering me?"

God has done His part; He has given us the Word. For example, the Lord doesn't give us money directly. **Deuteronomy 8:18** says that the Lord gives us the power to get wealth. The power is in His promises, His Word. As we plant those promises in our hearts, the truth of His Word germinates, and prosperity comes.

Healing operates the same way. There are numerous Scriptures that get the point across that God's Word is health to all our flesh. Here's two:

> *"For they are life unto those that find them, and health to all their flesh."* (**Prov. 4:22**)

> *"He sent his word, and healed them, and delivered them from their destructions."* (**Ps. 107:20**)

As discussed earlier, a person can get healed without planting God's Word in his or her heart. It comes through the prayers of others with the gifts of healing (**1 Cor. 12:9**), but it is not God's best. We should never be too proud to ask for help. The proper way to get healed is to take God's promises of healing and plant them in our hearts until they release their life-giving power into our physical bodies.

This law of seedtime and harvest operates in every area of our lives. If we will plant God's Word in our hearts, then allow the seed to germinate and the plant to grow to maturity, we will reap the fruit of a harvest. That is God's best!

Most people expect God's Word to work like a stick of dynamite, but God's Word is like a seed. We know that because of what Jesus said. Jesus said His words are alive. They contain life. The words in the Bible may look lifeless and powerless. Seeds do, too. But they are not without life or power.

In **Mark 4:30-31,** Jesus explained that the kingdom of God works like a seed. So, if we are to understand God's kingdom and how He operates, we need to understand seeds.

• A SEED IS ALIVE AND CONTAINS LIFE

Your physical senses are incapable of judging whether a seed is alive or not. You cannot see, feel, hear, smell, or taste the life in a seed. There is only one way to prove a seed is alive — plant it.

• A SEED DOES NOTHING UNTIL PLANTED

Seeds do not grow sitting in a sack on your shelf. They must be planted in the proper place. If you desire the Word of God to produce in your life, you must decide to plant the Word in your heart and mind.

The best way to plant the seed of God's Word in your life is by speaking the Word. Hearing others speak the Word is good but will not produce as bountiful a harvest as speaking the Word yourself. Your healing is *voice activated*.

Speaking God's Word with your mouth is essential. As we speak God's Word, we are planting the seed in our heart for the harvest of results we desire.

- **A SEED IS MUCH SMALLER THAN THE PLANT IT PRODUCES**

The problem you face may seem huge. In comparison, speaking God's Word aloud may seem too small. But when planted, that Word will grow in you and overcome the problem.

- **A SEED TAKES TIME TO PRODUCE**

No one expects a seed to produce a harvest the same day it is planted. Sometimes the Word of God seems to spring up and bear fruit immediately. Yet, if we knew the details, we would understand that the fruit of the Word grew in that person's life over time.

- **A SEED IS PERSISTENT**

A seed never gives up but works day and night. Even when you are sleeping, the seed you have planted is working to grow and express itself in a fruitful harvest.

- **A SEED WILL STOP GROWING WITHOUT NOURISHMENT**

Planting a seed is not enough to assure a harvest. Seeds must be protected and taken care of until harvest time. A seed which is dug up or not watered will not produce.

•More seeds planted produce a larger harvest

The parable of the sower relates to the spreading of the gospel and to any promise of God. For example, when the Word tells us that God will provide for our needs and to walk by faith and not by sight, these words are incorruptible seeds, ready to produce a great harvest. As we read, they are cast upon our heart and mind. If they are readily welcomed on fertile ground and accepted by faith, they are guaranteed to produce fruit. But if they are cast on a hard heart and mind that has surrendered to doubt, worry, and fear, no fruit is produced. Some cast God's Word on a hard heart every day and wonder why they reap no benefits.

The point is, God's Word is perfect, beyond corruption, and is to be treasured. It is guaranteed to produce a great harvest when cast on fertile soil. Once we believe this, we can break up the hard ground and prepare the soil for deep fertile planting.

Prayer for Healing

Lord, help me to cast aside all doubt and to trust, believe, and do what Your Word states in all areas of my life. Help me, Holy Spirit, to expect a great harvest in my life as together, we prepare the soil of my heart and mind for God's incorruptible seed. Amen.

Study, Meditate, Believe, and Speak God's Word

Lesson 2

God's Will is Healing

If I do not do the works of My Father, do not believe Me; but if I do, though you do not believe Me, believe the works.

John 10:37

WHEN WE EXAMINE the life of Jesus, one thing becomes clear; He met every dark situation of sin, sickness, disease, and demonic oppression with a healing solution. Jesus never gave a religious excuse for the problem. He always settled the issue by demonstrating what the Father's will looked like. It's also important to see that even when there was weak faith, He still brought a miracle.

Jesus never withheld a miracle, even when He was disappointed at weak faith. Some Christians will often tell someone they didn't get a healing or a miracle because their faith is small. Jesus never did that. It's always God's will to heal and deliver! The truth is that unbelief is what stops miracles and healings.

Believing and Speaking God's Word

Jesus Himself used the Word of God when confronted with the devil, saying, *"It is written..."* (**Matt. 4:2**).

God's Word is forever settled in heaven, but believers must settle God's Word on Earth. God's Word is always overflowing with power. It's only powerless when unspoken. Many people are defeated by what they believe and confess.

God's Word and Will

Matthew 12:34-37, *"For out of the abundance of the heart the mouth speaks. A good man out of the good treasure of his heart brings forth good things, and an evil man out of the evil treasure brings forth evil things. But I say to you that for every idle word men may speak, they will give account of it in the day of judgment. For by your words you will be justified, and by your words you will be condemned."*

The ministry of Jesus not only revealed God's heart of love for mankind's need for a Redeemer, but also unveiled His compassion for mankind's need for a Healer. The will of God was perfectly manifested in Jesus. Believers are to seek ways to fully act on that perfect revelation.

Just as the fall of man introduced sickness onto the earth as part of the curse, the cross of Christ has opened a door to healing as part of salvation's provision.

Healing is God's manifest power to restore broken hearts, broken lives, and broken bodies. Christ's blood at the cross removes all sin; His stripes at the whipping post provide healing in every dimension of our need.

Man's Dominion

> **Genesis 1:26,** *"And God said, let us make man in our image, after our likeness; and let them have dominion over the fish of the sea, and over the fowl of the air, and over the cattle, and over all the earth, and over every creeping thing that creeps on the earth."*

Using Your Spiritual Authority

There are many aspects to being a Christian. Some aspects of our identity in Christ we won't fully understand until we study God's Word about what it means to be a new creation in Christ (**2 Cor. 5:17**). We have privileges others don't have. When situations rise up against us, we don't have to tolerate them helplessly. We defeat trouble not with our own power, but by standing on the authority our heavenly Father has given us.

The word *aspect* is significant because until we realize who we really are, we're still diamonds in the rough.

> *"We can rejoice, too, when we run into problems and trials, for we know that they help us develop endurance. And endurance develops strength of character, and character strengthens our confident hope of salvation. And this hope will not lead to disappointment. For we know how dearly God loves us, because he has given us the Holy Spirit to fill our hearts with his love"* (**Rom. 5:3-5, NLT**).

When we're going through something, the Holy Spirit continues to lead us and point out to us the specifics of what we've been empowered to do.

Power is the ability to get results, and Jesus gave this power to His disciples. *"And when he had called unto him his twelve disciples, he gave them power against unclean spirits, to cast them out, and to heal all manner of sickness and all manner of disease"* (**Matt. 10:1**). We have that same power; therefore, we must learn how to apply it. As believers, we have the right to command and to use what God gave us to defeat the enemy.

We have what the world doesn't have. What has been given to us allows us to be victorious in our spiritual fight against the devil, no matter what happens. We're not powerless victims of circumstance. *"Behold, I give unto you power to tread on serpents and scorpions, and over all the power of the enemy: and nothing shall by any means hurt you.*

Notwithstanding in this rejoice not, that the spirits are subject unto you; but rather rejoice, because your names are written in heaven" (**Luke 10:19-20**).

We rejoice not simply because we have this power, but because our close, personal relationship with Jesus Christ gives us the same authority that He has.

We shouldn't be talking to God about the problem; we should instead be talking to the problem about God. Religion would have us ask Him to do something He's already done, but this is useless. The authority He gave us to deal with the issue is irrevocable; He won't go back on His Word. *"My covenant I will not break, nor alter the word that has gone out of My lips"* (**Ps. 89:34**).

We're more powerful than we realize, and we've been authorized to "flip the switch" ourselves.

Total trust in God and submission to Him puts us in touch with this awesome power. The spiritual authority on which we stand is stronger than granite because it comes from Him. We grasp it by the faith found in John 10. *"So be subject to God. Resist the devil [stand firm against him], and he will flee from you"* (**James 4:7, AMPC**). Neither the devil nor anything that comes from him can ever withstand the Word of God. Fully believing this is what sets us apart from others.

Healing is God's Will

How do we find the will of God? We find it in the Word of God, and that's another way of saying "Jesus."

The Word of God reveals to us the will of God. Jesus said, *"I didn't come of Myself, but He sent Me."* He said, *"I don't speak of Myself."* What does that mean? Everything you ever saw Jesus do or heard Him say was a direct revelation of the unchanging will of God for all men, for all time. So, when we read about the man full of leprosy in Luke 5:12-13 who came and said, *"Lord, I know You can do it, if You will,"* and Jesus reached out, put His hand on the man's sick body, and said, *"I will,"* does it mean anything to us?

The Bible says that if everything Jesus said and did was recorded, not even the world itself could contain all of the books that should be written (**John 21:25**). We have a very, very small amount of what He said and did recorded, and this amount was hand-picked by God the Father, and manifested through His holy men.

Why did He pen this? Because this Word is a historical, accurate account, but it is much, much more than history. It's God speaking to all mankind, revealing His will for everyone for all time. If the man's healing had just been for him, it wouldn't have been in the Bible where you and I could read it and believe it today. The fact that it's there and that it's written and recorded in numerous places means we are supposed to take it how?

When He said, *"I will,"* that's not just *"I will"* to that man on that day. That is the unchanging will of God for all men for all time. When He said, *"I will,"* to him and had it recorded in the Bible, it's an *"I will"* to you and to me.

Why do we still have millions of people begging God to heal them, and saying, "If it would be His will." We might ask, "Well, how would you know it is God's will?" They would reply, "When I'm healed." "Do you mean when you see it, you'll believe it?" "Yes."

It will be too late to believe it. It will be too late for faith. If you have to see it before you're going to believe it is His will, then you are refusing to have any faith. Faith believes it when it does not look like it's even possible, just simply because He said it. God's will is to heal. Look at **Luke 5:12-13** again. The man said, *"If you will, I know you can."* Jesus said, *"I will."* In verses 12 and 13 of the Living Bible, the man said, *"Sir, if you only will, you can clear me of every trace of my disease. Jesus reached out and touched the man and said, 'Of course I will. Be healed.' And the leprosy left him instantly."*

Draining Doubt and Unbelief

Jesus answered a powerful question from His disciples when they could not heal someone. He said because of your *unbelief*. We must limit the amount of unbelief we let in, from TV and computer, if we want to receive supernatural healing and miracles.

> *And when they had come to the multitude, a man came to Him, kneeling down to Him and saying, "Lord, have mercy on my son, for he is an epileptic and suffers severely; for he often falls into the fire and often into the water. So I brought*

him to Your disciples, but they could not cure him." Then Jesus answered and said, "O faithless and perverse generation, how long shall I be with you? How long shall I bear with you? Bring him here to Me." And Jesus rebuked the demon, and it came out of him; and the child was cured from that very hour. Then the disciples came to Jesus privately and said, "Why could we not cast it out?" So Jesus said to them, "Because of your unbelief; for assuredly, I say to you, if you have faith as a mustard seed, you will say to this mountain, 'Move from here to there,' and it will move; and nothing will be impossible for you (**Matthew 17:14-20**).

Prayer For Healing

Lord, in Your name I cast out devils from my life and boldly receive the abundant life that You gave me. I speak directly to every mountain of satanic adversity—sin, sickness, demons, fear, and poverty. I cast you out in the mighty name of Jesus. (**John 10:10; Mark 16:17; Mark 11:23**)

How Confession Helps

The amount of time we spend praising God is the greatest single indicator of where we are in our relationship with Him. Everything starts from this relationship. Praising God strengthens and builds our faith. There is power in our words when they agree with God's Word. God spoke the universe into existence by His Word. As believers, we have been given that same power and authority to create change in the world by confessing God's Word.

Man-made Religious Traditions

> "God is in control of everything." This has become a strong belief of believers and unbelievers. It's not true! It's another way of saying, "Whatever happens—good or bad — is the will of God."

According to the Scriptures, God is in overall control, but He has delegated authority and dominion of the earth to people. The spiritual laws of sowing and reaping, free will, binding and loosing, resisting the devil, speaking the name of Jesus, and believing are in the control of people. **Psalm 115:16**, *"The heaven, even the heavens, are the LORD's; But the earth He has given to the children of men."*

Divine Healing Truth

1. A false tradition in many churches tries to make the Scripture say that God uses sickness to chastise those He loves. The truth is that God is a Spirit, and He chastises (instructs, trains, teaches) with His Word. Proof can be found in **2 Timothy 3:16,**

> *"All Scripture is given by inspiration of God, and is profitable for doctrine, for reproof, for correction, for instruction in righteousness."*

2. Christ was *made* to be sin for us when He bore our sins. He was *made* a curse for us when He bore our sicknesses.

3. Christ never refused those who followed Him for healing. Repeatedly, the gospels tell us that He "healed them all." Christ is the healer, and He has never changed.

4. Only one person in all of Scripture asked for healing by saying, *"If it be your will."* That was the leper to who Jesus immediately responded, *"I will; be clean."* (**Luke 5:12-13**.)

Lesson 3

Natural Knowledge vs. Revelation Knowledge

That the God of our Lord Jesus Christ, the Father of glory, may give unto you the spirit of wisdom and revelation in the knowledge of him:

Ephesians 1:17

I'm very fortunate to have had some wonderful Bible teaching when I was first born again. One of these teachers used to say, "I know that I know that I know—way down deep in my knower." It's probably not the best grammar, but it was a revelation to me!

You see, I caught the meaning. There is natural knowledge, but then there is a knowledge that comes from the inside out of your spirit, not your brain. You can have knowledge of some great Bible promises and believe them, but until you have revelation knowledge about **1 Peter 2:24**, it will be tough to receive the supernatural healing that God wants for you on your own faith.

A lack of revelation knowledge is the greatest cause of faith failures.

Most Christians believe the Word of God with their brains, but they haven't meditated on it enough for it to "light up" in their hearts. If they had, that Word would absolutely revolutionize their lives. Nothing would be able to shake them loose from it.

In the kingdom of God, there is a knowing that comes from the inside out, rather than the outside in. It comes directly from God to our spirit. Here, we're offering a more in-depth answer to the question, what is *revelation knowledge?*

1. The Rock on Which the Church is Built

> *"On this rock I will build My church, and the gates of Hades shall not prevail against it."* **Matthew 16:18**

In this verse, Jesus was speaking to Peter, whose name means "rock" or "stone." But we know that Jesus did not build His church upon one man. So, what is the rock to which He was referring?

He was referring to the rock of *revelation knowledge.*

Just before this statement, Jesus had asked the disciples, *"Who do you say I am?"* Peter answered Him by declaring, *"You are the Christ, the Son of the living God"* (**Matthew 16:16**). *"Blessed are you, Simon…"* Jesus responded, *"because flesh and blood has not revealed this to you, but My Father who is in heaven"* (**Matthew 16:17, NASB**).

In other words, Jesus was saying, "Peter, you didn't learn this information through your physical senses. You received it another way. You received it directly from God."

That is how we, as the church, are to operate in our everyday lives—through a knowledge that comes only from God. Anything we can learn in the natural is incomparable to it, and when it comes, it changes things. It makes you see old things in an entirely new light. It gives you such unshakable confidence that, as Jesus said to Peter, *"The gates of hell cannot prevail against you"* (see verse 18).

But revelations like that aren't cheap to come by. You must meditate on the Word and search the Spirit of God for them because they are "hidden" in Him. The Bible says God has hidden His wisdom for the saints (**1 Cor. 2:7-9**). Notice, He's hidden it *for* you, not *from* you. He wants you to have it.

Don't think, however, that God is just going to drop great revelations into your lap while you're watching television. You must seek Him. If you're hungry for revelation knowledge, get yourself in a position to receive it by meditating on the Word, and praying and fellowshipping with the Lord. Begin to receive those revelations from Him.

It's the most exciting kind of learning there is!

2. The Truth that Sets You Free

"You will know the truth and the truth will set you free." **John 8:32**

Revelation knowledge is not a list of facts or trivia. It has deep power—the power to set you free and elevate you to victories you never imagined possible.

There are a lot of "facts" floating around, which are, more often than not, a set of good guesses or opinions that change with the wind. Prideful people think they know much, but humble people, hungry for revelation, realize they need the Creator and Savior to access truth.

Revelation knowledge is the only way to win the battle for truth. Satan is ever-present, spewing lies day and night in hopes that someone will latch onto them and give him total access to their lives. Jesus said he is a liar and the father of it. That's why we need revelation knowledge, which is revealed truth.

You will know the truth, and the truth will make you free. The truth that you're healed will always make you free from sickness and disease.

3. Spirit, Soul, and Body in the Right Order

> *"It is the Spirit who gives life; the flesh is no help at all."* **John 6:63 (ESV)**

You are a spirit with a soul who lives in a physical body. The body—the flesh—is the most demanding of them all, but revelation knowledge comes from putting spirit, soul, and body in that order (**1 Thess. 5:23**).

When you were born again, it was not your physical body that was transformed, but your spirit. That is who you are. Your physical body is just what houses your spirit. God is a spirit being, and we were made in His image. You live in your body, but no one can see the real you—your spirit. That's why they call the body "the remains" because that's all that remains on the earth of you when you die. The born-again spirit goes to heaven.

God's Word says the outward man—the flesh—is decaying every day, but the spirit is renewing every day (**2 Cor. 4:16**). The body is dying a little each day, but by believing what **Romans 8:11** says, you can arrest that death process.

It's essential to put our spirit man ahead of all else to receive revelation knowledge. **Hebrews 4:12** tells us the Word of God separates the soul from the spirit. God is a Spirit, and that's why we must worship God in spirit, not merely in soul or body (**John 4:24**).

That's why when you pray in the spirit, knowledge comes to you that you did not know in your mind—revelation knowledge. Praying in the spirit is one way to put spirit, soul, and body in the proper order. You are setting aside your own natural thoughts and seeking after the voice of the Holy Spirit.

4. The Key to Your Victory

> *"This Book of the Law shall not depart from your mouth, but you shall meditate on it day and night, so that you may be careful to do according to all that is written in it. For then*

you will make your way prosperous, and then you will have good success." **Joshua 1:8 (ESV)**

How did David–a shepherd boy–become so strong in spirit that God chose him to be king of Israel?

The answer is simple: revelation knowledge.

That's what turned David into such a spiritual powerhouse–revelation that came to him through hours of thinking about the things of God. You can almost imagine the day he wrote **Psalm 23**, that he was just sitting, singing praises to God, and meditating on His goodness. He was just fellowshipping with Him when suddenly, the anointing of the Lord came upon him, and he said, "The Lord is *my* Shepherd!"

He then thought about the sheep he watched over as a boy. I faced death for those sheep. I led them where pastures were green, and waters were cool, clean, deep, and peaceful. He kept meditating on that until it started to thrill him. When the lion and the bear came, didn't God prepare a table before me in the presence of those enemies? He gave me victory. My God! My God will fight for me. The Lord is my Shepherd! I shall not want!

That revelation welled up in David so strong that the devil couldn't beat it out of him. So, when Goliath tried to make a fool out of Israel, David went after him. Goliath was able to scare off everyone else, but he couldn't shake David because he had a revelation inside him that said, *Yea, though I walk through the valley of the shadow of death, I will fear no evil: for my God is with me.* **Psalm 23:4**

That revelation enabled David to say, *"I come against you in the name of the Lord of Hosts"* (**1 Samuel 17:45**). He then sent a rock sailing into that giant's brain.

That's what revelation knowledge will do for you, too. It's the key to your victory. Whenever the devil comes to attack, if you hit him with the rock of revelation knowledge, you'll knock him flat every time.

Determine right now that you're going to meditate the Word until you begin receiving revelation knowledge. Keep that Word before you until you receive a revelation of Jesus as your Healer or your Deliverer or your Financier—whatever you need Him to be. Don't settle for a shallow mental understanding of Him. Get a deep revelation, and His grace *will* be multiplied to you!

How to Access Revelation Knowledge for Any Situation

No matter what you're facing today, there is an answer. It may not seem like it, but it's true. God has provided the knowledge and direction you need to come out on the other side of this better than you could ever ask or imagine. Here, I will share how to access revelation knowledge for any situation so you can find the answers you need!

1. **Meditate on Specific Scriptures**–This may seem obvious, but mental knowledge of God's Word isn't enough. Even the devil can quote it! Revelation knowledge comes when you've spent

time meditating on specific Scriptures that relate to your situation. When you've read a particular verse over and over, it can be easy to gloss over it without stopping to examine it. Pause and allow the Lord to show you a deeper meaning than you've ever known. He'll show you how to apply it directly to your current situation. Remember, revelation knowledge comes from the inside out, not the outside in. As you meditate on His Word, be sure you open your heart and mind for a fresh word and leave religious tradition or your own preconceived ideas aside.

2. **Pray in the Spirit**—We are spirit beings with a soul and a body, but to receive revelation knowledge, we have to tap into the secret place. Praying in the spirit makes you smarter than yourself. That sums it up! When you don't have the answer, the Holy Spirit will quicken it to your spirit when you pray in your heavenly language. If you need an answer to a particular problem, increase the time you normally spend praying in the spirit and continue until you hear from Him.

3. **Listen**—You haven't finished praying until you've *listened*. It's easy to rattle off our wish lists or complaints to the Lord, then go along our merry way, but that isn't going to get it done. It's in listening that the Holy Spirit is able to bring witty ideas and fresh revelation to our spirits. I heard of a man who knew how to listen for revelation in such a way that he went from poverty

to becoming a multimillionaire just from the time he spent in his closet listening to the Lord.

4. **Listen to Teachings**–God will often speak to you through His ministers in supernatural ways. Even teachings that are decades old can provide a revelation about your finances, your healing, your relationships, or any other area where you need answers. This is another way to mediate on Scriptures, like we talked about in the first step. Praise God for the body of Christ. We can learn through the revelation of others and quicken our own revelation.

5. **Fast**–When people like Ezra, Esther, Paul, and Barnabas needed answers from God, they turned to the power of fasting. A fast doesn't change God; it changes you! It is a clearing away of the flesh and an opening of the heart to hear from the Holy Spirit.

Whatever you're facing today, *there is an answer*. Not just any answer, either–a perfect one! God desires to help you achieve the desires of your heart and live victoriously. Revelation knowledge is His way of getting the answers to you. Don't let it pass you by! Use these five steps and press in until you hear from Him.

Prayer for Healing

Lord, I'm so thankful my spirit is complete in Christ. The Spirit in me gives life to my body. And I'm thankful that no weapon formed against me will prosper. (**Col. 2:9-10; Isa. 54:17; Rom. 8:11**)

How Confession Helps

Your confession (profession) is the words you believe and speak every day. Confession brings possession, whether positive or negative. Your mouth is the link between having the things God has promised you or living without them. If you desire to experience God's provision in every area of your life, begin today to speak and pray the promises found in God's Word. Your confession that agrees with God guarantees successful results every time!

Man-made Religious Tradition

"You never know what God is going to do." I really believe we create sayings like this one as an excuse for why we didn't receive one of the promises of God. Man-made sayings become religious traditions. Jesus said that your religious tradition will nullify the promise of God in your life (see **Mark 7:13**). The truth is that we can know what God is going to do because He is going to *"watch over His Word to perform it"* (**Jer. 1:12**).

Some pastors and teachers refer to **1 Corinthians 2:9** to say that we cannot know the plans of God. *"Eye has not seen, nor ear heard, Nor have entered into the heart of man The things which God has prepared for those who love Him."* This quotation is incomplete and it's taken out of context. If preachers would keep reading, the Scripture says that God will reveal His plans to us by His Spirit!

Building Faith for Healing

> *"For in it the righteousness of God is revealed from faith to faith; as it is written, "The just shall live by faith."*
> **Romans 1:17**

- Faith pleases God, receives answers to prayer, and gives peace, joy, gifts of the Spirit, and miracles.

- Faith will defeat sin, sickness, trouble, depression, fear, doubt, worry, demons, and sadness.

Divine Healing Truth

1. The truth is that healing has already been provided by the finished work of Jesus.

2. Mankind is a triune being–spirit, soul, and body. We do not glorify God in our spirit by continuing in sin. We do not glorify God by remaining sick.

3. God's Word is His will. God's promises and the life of Christ reveal God's will.

4. If healing is not for everyone, Christ should have qualified His promise when He said, *"Whatever you desire when you pray – believe that you receive it and you will have it"* **Mark 11:24**.

Lesson 4

Healing Belongs to You

Who his own self bare our sins in his own body on the tree, that we, being dead to sins, should live unto righteousness: by whose stripes ye were healed.

1 Peter 2:24

Faith in God and faith in God's Word are always required for divine healing. Faith will be on the part of the person who is praying for someone or faith on the part of the one receiving. The absolute truth is that there is amazing power in having faith in God's Word. It isn't just information on a page in the Bible. His Word is *health* and *healing* to anyone who will choose to believe it.

The regular study of God's Word is like taking spiritual vitamins. It will build your spiritual, mental, emotional, and physical immune system, resulting in the ability to walk in divine health and overcome sickness and disease!

If you are presently sick, God's Word is health to your body and mind. Reading, hearing, choosing to believe it, and act upon it is the spiritual equivalent to taking medicine (**Prov. 4:20-22**). God's medicine always works against any sickness, disease, or ailment!

> *"For I will restore you to health And I will heal you of your wounds,' declares the LORD"* (**Jer.30:17a**). **Isaiah 53:4,** *"Surely He has borne our sicknesses, and carried our diseases; yet we did esteem Him stricken, smitten of God, and afflicted."*

This means that the pains and sicknesses that you are experiencing were laid on Jesus. Jesus bore them just as He bore your sins. The Lord God actually laid your sins, sicknesses, sorrows, and weaknesses upon Jesus so you wouldn't have to bear them yourself. It's a gift! Healing is yours right now. *"He made Him sin with your sins that you might be the righteousness of God in Christ"* (**2 Cor. 5:21**). He made Jesus sick with your diseases that you might be healed and whole in Christ.

Healing and Salvation

God's loving, healing provision of salvation is rooted in the redemptive, finished work of Jesus. By nature, God is a healing God. In terms of power, there is nothing impossible for Him. Legally, the finished work of Christ opens the door for a holy God to show His healing mercy to a people who, by their sinful nature, would be unqualified to receive His healing touch.

Anyone Can Be Healed

Matthew 9:35

"Jesus went about all the cities and villages, teaching in their synagogues, preaching the gospel of the kingdom, and healing every sickness and every disease among the people."

Acts 5:12-16

"Through the hands of the apostles many signs and wonders were done among the people. And they were all with one accord in Solomon's Porch. Yet none of the rest dared join them, but the people esteemed them highly. And believers were increasingly added to the Lord, multitudes of both men and women, so that they brought the sick out into the streets and laid them on beds and couches, that at least the shadow of Peter passing by might fall on some of them. Also, a multitude gathered from the surrounding cities to Jerusalem, bringing sick people and those who were tormented by unclean spirits, and they were all healed."

Both salvation and healing have already been purchased by Jesus at the cross and the whipping post. It's a done deal for anyone in the world. Your healing and your right standing with God already exist in the unseen kingdom realm. Believers can receive it by faith for themselves. They can also lay hands on others by faith, and those they touch will recover.

Jesus the Healer

Good health is something we all want, but few people know its ultimate source. Healing doesn't come from prescriptions, doctors, hospitals, or even from eating right and living a healthy lifestyle. In these end times, many people are depending on these things because of a widespread fear of getting sick, but it doesn't have to be that way. There is an antidote to all sickness and disease, and His name is Jesus.

Often, just the thought of "something going around" can make people panic and behave irrationally. The world's prevailing mindset is one of hopeless resignation; this way of thinking is indicative of a world that doesn't know God. We have specific, detailed promises regarding the protection He provides against diseases. Trusting Him in this area gives us peace of mind, no matter what we see going on around us.

> *"For he will rescue you from every trap and protect you from deadly disease. He will cover you with his feathers. He will shelter you with his wings. His faithful promises are your armor and protection. Do not be afraid of the terrors of the night, nor the arrow that flies in the day. Do not dread the disease that stalks in darkness, nor the disaster that strikes at midday. Though a thousand fall at your side, though ten*

thousand are dying around you, these evils will not touch you." **Psalms 91:3-7 (NLT)**

There's nothing wrong with taking preventive health care measures, seeing doctors when necessary, and using common sense; however, despite their good intentions, there's only so much doctors can do through their own efforts. Wise physicians pray because they know the power of believing in the Great Physician. Jesus went to the cross to provide healing for us on every level. "*…By his wounds you are healed*" (**1 Peter 2:24, NLT**).

God loves us, and sickness isn't His will for us. If we really believe this, we won't let fear carry us away. His promise of protection, given thousands of years ago, still stands today. "*Yea, though I walk through the valley of the shadow of death, I will fear no evil: for thou art with me; thy rod and thy staff they comfort me*" (**Ps. 23:4**). Those who trust in Him have nothing to fear.

Healing was a large part of Jesus's earthly ministry. All that was necessary to be healed was belief that He was willing and able to do so. Trust in Jesus allowed Him to heal anyone who came to Him (**Matt. 9:20-22; Matt. 12:22; Mark 1:40-45; Luke 17:11-19**). God's promises of healing, both physically and emotionally, haven't changed at all.

What's worse than any disease is the fear it causes in those who don't have a relationship with Christ. Knowing Him and constantly being in His presence keeps us shielded from this debilitating emotion. "*For God hath not given us the spirit of fear; but of power, and of love, and of a sound mind"* (**2 Tim. 1:7**). There's an enemy loose in the world intent on spreading fear and panic; taking refuge in God in the midst of the situation keeps us safe.

We can place complete trust in God's Word on healing. It's the absolute truth. *"God is not a man, that he should lie; neither the son of man, that he should repent: hath he said, and shall he not do it? or hath he spoken, and shall he not make it good?"* (**Num. 23:19**). In a topsy-turvy world filled with confusion and uncertainty, reliance on God's promises of wholeness and soundness gives us peace.

Prayer for Healing

> *Lord, You have taken my sicknesses and carried my sorrows, sin, disease, and pains. By Your stripes, I am healed* (**Isa. 53:4-5; 1 Peter 2:24; Matt. 8:17**).

How Confession Helps

Faith-filled words will help you overcome. Fear-filled words will bring defeat. The words you speak every day are your confession. Your confession will put you *over* or put you *under* the circumstances.

Man-made Religious Traditions

"Whatever happens must be God's will." This religious tradition also says if it wasn't God's will, He wouldn't have allowed it to happen. Not true! God's will is not always done on Earth. Just listen to the news broadcasts. People are choosing to live their lives in total opposition of God's will.

Divine Healing Truth

1. Satan is always bad. God is always good. Sickness is from Satan. Health and healing always comes from God.

2. Satan's work is always to kill. Christ's work is always to give life.

3. All authority and power over disease and devils belongs to Jesus, and Jesus gave His authority to every believer to use in His name.

Believe God and Act in Agreement with His Word

Lesson 5

Receive Communion

The Lord Jesus on the same night in which He was betrayed took bread; and when He had given thanks, He broke it and said, "Take, eat; this is My body which is broken for you; do this in remembrance of Me."

1 Corinthians 11:23-24

When we receive communion in a worthy manner–honoring, respectful, worshipful–we're promised a strong, healthy, and long life (see **1 Cor. 11:29-30**).

Healing Comes from Christ

WITH OUR BUSY lives and the constant demands on our time, health is something we rarely stop to think about. We may take for granted that our bodies will always work the way they're supposed to. Even when we fall ill with something, we expect to eventually be healthy again, and we're grateful for our recovery. However, those of us who look past the doctors and medicines know who the true source of healing is.

There's nothing wrong with consulting physicians, but as limited human beings, there's only so much they can do. They can promote healing, but they aren't the source of it; healing only comes from Jesus the Christ. There have been instances when doctors were forced to admit there was nothing more that could be done for someone who was terminally ill; however, things change when God gets involved in the situation. *"Then they cried out to the LORD in their trouble, And He saved them out of their distresses. He sent His word and healed them And delivered them from their destructions"* (**Ps. 107:19-20**).

God's will is found in His Word, and healing is His will for us. He loves us and wants the best for us; sickness and health issues don't figure into the equation. During Jesus's ministry, when a leper wondered if healing was His will, Jesus's response was swift and direct. *"And behold, a leper came and worshiped Him, saying, 'Lord, if You are willing, You can make me clean.' Then Jesus put out His hand and touched him, saying, 'I am willing; be cleansed.' Immediately his leprosy was cleansed"* (**Matt. 8:2-3**).

Jesus healed plenty of others, as well. *"When evening had come, they brought to Him many who were demon-possessed. And He cast out the spirits with a word and healed all who were sick"* (**Matt. 8:16**). None of those who were healed were perfect; the only requirement to receive healing was believing in His ability to heal. When we're struggling with health issues, we may have the mistaken notion that our past mistakes disqualify us from receiving healing from Jesus. However, we should never minimize the power of believing that He wants us back in perfect health.

Some people think that they're sick because God is punishing them for something they did; that's wrong thinking. God isn't mad at us or out to "get" us. He wants to show us His mercy and compassion; restoring us to health that's even better than before has a way of getting our attention. *"And Jesus went forth, and saw a great multitude, and was moved with compassion toward them, and he healed their sick"* (**Matt. 14:14**). Jesus healed then, and He's still healing now.

Doctors are committed to helping us get well, and God is well able to work through them; however, our faith shouldn't stop with their efforts to restore our health. Jesus easily healed the woman with the issue of blood after doctors had unsuccessfully tried to heal her. *"And, behold, a woman, which was diseased with an issue of blood twelve years, came behind him, and touched the hem of his garment: For she said within herself, If I may but touch his garment, I shall be whole. But Jesus turned him about, and when he saw her, he said, Daughter, be of good comfort; thy faith hath made thee whole. And the woman was made whole from that hour"* (**Matt. 9:20-22**). When trusting in doctors doesn't get the job done, faith in Jesus Christ, the Great Physician, never fails.

Nothing Missing, Nothing Broken

Most people think of healing from a physical standpoint in terms of the body recovering from an injury. That's certainly one facet of it, but there are other aspects of healing, as well. Our enemy, the devil, delights in stealing from us. Some of the things he tries to take away are our peace of mind and the sense of emotional stability and security that comes from trusting in Christ; however, he's no match for Jesus, who heals our emotions with one touch.

Wholeness, with nothing missing and nothing broken, is God's will for us. The enemy tries to steal our joy and everything else we value in our lives. God restores it. *"The thief cometh not, but for to steal, and to kill, and to destroy: I am come that they might have life, and that they might have it more abundantly"* (**John 10:10**).

During His ministry, Jesus healed and restored to perfect wholeness people who had faith in Him. This didn't just pertain to physical healing, but mental and emotional healing, as well. Once, He healed a man who had been possessed by evil spirits. *"And they come to Jesus, and see him that was possessed with the devil, and had the legion, sitting, and clothed, and in his right mind: and they were afraid"* (**Mark 5:15**). The enemy has no chance when he encounters Christ or a believer living with the authority given by Christ.

Healing also took place with the woman who asked Jesus to heal her daughter (**Matt. 15:28**) and the boy from who Jesus cast out demons before delivering him back to his father (**Luke 9:42, AMPC**). This kind of deliverance and complete recovery comes only from God. Jesus's coming to restore everything that was missing or broken was prophesied in the Old Testament. *"And nothing of theirs was lacking, either small or great, sons or daughters, spoil or anything which they had taken from* *them; David recovered all"* (**1 Sam. 30:19**). This was fulfilled in Jesus's death and resurrection.

A thorough knowledge of God's Word concerning healing and a willingness to stand on it whenever the devil shows up are effective weapons against his attacks. He uses every situation he can to highlight the negative aspects of things that happen in our lives in hopes of crumbling our trust in Jesus. Satan is a liar and a thief, but when this thief tries to steal what God wants us to have, we're empowered to stop him. *"People do not despise a thief if he steals to satisfy himself when he is starving. Yet when he is found, he must restore sevenfold; he may have to give up all the substance of his house"* (**Prov. 6:30-31**). When we realize what he's up to, we have authority to make him return everything he's stolen, and then some.

This authority is one of the results of the finished works of Jesus, the God of restoration. When Satan stole from Adam and Eve in the garden of Eden, Christ later came and restored the balance of power back to God's original plan. He also restored everything that the enemy had stolen or destroyed. *"And I will restore to you the years that the locust hath eaten, the cankerworm, and the caterpillar, and the palmerworm, my great army which I sent among you"* (**Joel 2:25**). We claim this restoration by faith.

Believers don't have to tolerate brokenness. The word *shalom* not only means peace, but also complete, intact, and in good health. Jesus is our peace, our healing, and our wholeness. For true healing and restoration on every level, He's our shalom.

Prayer for Healing

Lord, You forgive all my iniquities and heal all my diseases. You redeem my life from destruction (**Ps. 103:2-5**).

How Confession Helps

You were created in God's image and likeness, and you have the ability to choose and speak positive, faith-filled words just like God does. Your positive faith confession will help you see yourself the way God sees you.

Divine Healing Truth

1. In connection with the Lord's Supper, the cup is taken *in remembrance* of His blood which was shed for the *remission of our sins*. The bread is eaten *in remembrance* of His body on which was laid our diseases and the stripes by which *we are healed*.

2. Jesus always commissioned the preaching of the gospel by including healing of the sick. That command still applies to the ministry today!

3. It's dangerous to apply a teaching about God being sovereign. Many people believe God can do anything He wants whenever

He wants. Of course, God has the ability to do anything, but God has bound Himself with His Word. God will always cooperate with His own spiritual laws.

Lesson 6

By the Stripes of Jesus

But he was pierced for our transgressions, he was crushed for our iniquities the punishment that brought us peace was on him, and by his wounds we are healed.

Isaiah 53:5

Good health is an important component of the kind of life God wants for us. When we're healthy and strong both physically and emotionally, we're capable of handling what He wants us to do. The world doesn't know that it's God's will for us to be healed because it doesn't know *Him*; as a result, we see sickness and brokenness all around us. When we're sick, believing His promises about healing allows us to experience it firsthand.

Doctors are limited to what they learned in medical school, but wise physicians admit to miracles they can't take credit for or explain. Psychiatry and modern medicine are still learning about the relationship between the human spirit and the Holy Spirit, and the role faith plays in healing. However, studying the many miraculous healings Jesus performed during His ministry affirms supernatural realities. For those who believe, healing is imminent, despite what it may seem like at the moment. *"But to you who fear My name The Sun of Righteousness shall arise With healing in His wings; And you shall go out And grow fat like stall-fed calves"* (**Mal. 4:2**).

Careful analysis of those healings reveals that faith was the common denominator connecting the sick person to the power of God. When Jesus healed the woman suffering from a blood disorder despite all the doctors' efforts, her belief in His ability to restore health and wholeness was the key factor. All it took was one touch. *"For she said, If I may touch but his clothes, I shall be whole. And straightway the fountain of her blood was dried up; and she felt in her body that she was healed of that plague... And he said unto her, Daughter, thy faith hath made thee whole; go in peace and be whole of thy plague"* (**Mark 5:28-29, 34**). Choosing to trust Jesus restored her physically as well as emotionally.

Sickness is from the devil, and despite what some religious people say, sickness is not God's will. When we refuse to accept the world's philosophy and acknowledge the power of the Great Physician, we receive His favor. The Canaanite woman acted on her belief when she asked Jesus to heal her daughter, and He honored her faith. *"Then Jesus answered and said unto her, O woman, great is thy faith be it unto thee even as thou wilt. And her daughter was made whole from that very hour"* (**Matt. 15:28**).

Now here's something even more radical. We have that same healing power in us! God gave the power to Jesus who, through His grace and love, passed it on to us. *"Heal the sick, cleanse the lepers, raise the dead, cast out demons. Freely you have received, freely give"* (**Matt. 10:8**). We're not helpless, and we don't have to tolerate mental illness, depression, physical infirmities, or any other kind of evil tormenting us or our loved ones. Doctors have the best of intentions, but true healing begins in the spiritual realm.

Popular culture shouts at us that sickness inevitably overcomes good health as we get older; however, it doesn't have to be that way. God only wants good for us and choosing to have faith and act on what His Word says allows Him to establish His plans for us. *"It will be health to your flesh, And strength to your bones"* (**Prov. 3:8**). Our well-being hinges on what we believe.

Your Body Is Not Your Own

> "Do you not know that your body is the temple of the Holy Spirit *who is* in you, whom you have from God, and you are not your own? For you were bought at a price; therefore glorify God in your body and in your spirit, which are God's." **1 Corinthians 6:19-20**

You and I are the "overseers" living in the house (temple) that belongs to God. If this is true, and it is, we should respect and protect God's property in a way that we probably have not thought about before. Any demonic spirit bringing sickness, disease, or tragedy should be cast out in Jesus's name (**Mark 16:17**)!

Prayer for Healing

Lord, I attend to Your Word and submit myself to Your sayings. They are life to me and healing to my whole body. You have sent Your Word to heal me and deliver me from destruction (**Prov. 4:20-22**; **Ps. 107:20**).

How Confession Helps

From the Book of Hebrews, we know that Jesus is the High Priest of our confession. We also know that because Jesus is our High Priest, we should "hold fast" to our confession. From **1 Timothy**, we know that our confession is what will help when we fight a good fight of faith (**Heb. 3:1**; **Heb. 4:14**; **Heb. 10:23**; **1 Tim. 6:12-13**).

Man-made Religious Tradition

There are many man-made traditions that ultimately create doubt in the truth of God's Word about healing. One such tradition is that God does not cause sickness, but that He "allows" it. This statement is the same as saying that sickness is God's will. This is *not* true! God's will is always healing and blessing. It's up to believers to receive God's expressed will.

For example: If I own a vehicle and decide to let you drive it for a specified time and you wrecked it in a traffic accident, it's obvious that I did not cause the wreck. But it would be just as wrong to blame me as having "allowed" it.

Blood Covenant

God's Word and promises are far more powerful than our earthly contracts. When God makes a covenant, He guarantees it with His own blood (the blood of Jesus).

Divine Healing Truth

1. The Scriptures teach that the Spirit's work is to quicken, or make alive, our mortal bodies in this life (**Rom. 8:11**).

2. Jesus declared that a sick woman was bound by Satan and ought to be loosed. He cast out the spirit of infirmity, and she was healed (**Luke 13:11**).

3. A devil which possessed a man was the cause of him being blind and dumb. When the devil was cast out, the man could both see and talk (**Matt. 12:22**).

Lesson 7

Enter into Rest

For indeed the gospel was preached to us as well as to them;
but the word which they heard did not profit them,
not being mixed with faith in those who heard it.
For we who have believed do enter that rest.

Hebrews 4:2-3

Those who believe are at rest, trusting in God's promises.

Enjoying good health is something believers can take for granted, but a glance around us reveals that not everyone is walking in this blessing. Religion doesn't understand the difference between the covenants of the law and of grace; it teaches people to beg and plead for God to heal them. It's important that we see healing under the correct covenant. We no longer must pray for it; we're thankful for it because we're already healed.

What was true under the law may not be true under grace. Under the law, sickness and disease were part of the curse. Healing has already been made available to us, but back then, the people had to ask God for it. *"Heal me, O LORD, and I shall be healed; save me, and I shall be saved: for thou art my praise"* (**Jer. 17:14**). This was a valid prayer under the law, but it isn't now.

In the Old Testament, God promised what He would do; healing was part of the promise. *"Behold, I will bring it health and cure, and I will cure them, and will reveal unto them the abundance of peace and truth"* (**Jer. 33:6**); however, Mosaic law was based on what the people did first, before God could do anything. To be healthy was a blessing, and the people had to work hard to earn every blessing they could.

The cross of Christ changed the requirements for healing. Under the old covenant, healing only happened through the people's regular animal sacrifices as atonement for their failure to keep the law through their own efforts. When Jesus came, many neither understood nor accepted the link between faith in Him and healing, despite being shown miracles (**John 9:1-38**). When He died, the Old Testament prophecy was fulfilled. *"But he was wounded for our transgressions, he was bruised for our iniquities: the chastisement of our peace was upon him; and with his stripes we are healed"* (**Isa. 53:5**).

It's significant that this says we are healed, not that we "will be" healed. Renewing our minds according to the finished works of Jesus Christ reminds us that healing is available to us, no matter what the doctor says. The world tells us we must accept ill-health and resign ourselves to it, but God's Word tells us otherwise. *"Beloved, I wish above all things that thou mayest prosper and be in health, even as thy soul prospereth"*

(3 John 1:2). Healing is God's will for us. Nothing the world says can ever change what He has already said and done..

When Jesus took away the curses of sickness and disease, He left all of the blessings of strength, vitality, and abundant good health. All we need to do is accept those blessings by faith. The world still struggles with health issues, both emotional and physical, because it doesn't understand how healing works under the covenant of grace. If we still struggle with these issues, it may be because we've become absent-minded in this area. *"Bless the LORD, O my soul, And forget not all His benefits: Who forgives all your iniquities, Who heals all your diseases"* **(Ps. 103:2-3)**.

The gift of perfect health has been presented. *"Whatever is good and perfect is a gift coming down to us from God our Father, who created all the lights in the heavens"* **(James 1:17, NLT)**. Our healing is already waiting for us to receive it; we can't help but be thankful when we reflect on this. We are the healed, on every level.

God's Healing Touch

Good health is something many of us take for granted and never think about until we get sick. When that happens, we've gotten in the habit of reaching for medication or seeing a doctor for relief. There's nothing wrong with that, but believers must not forget the origins of true healing. A sound mind and a healthy body keep us operating at peak efficiency; these are blessings from God.

Wise doctors ask the Great Physician to work through them because they know that there are some things that even they can't fix. Healing is more than just writing prescriptions and performing surgery. The world's medical and psychological communities now admit to the powerful effect the mind has on healing. This is confirmed in God's Word. *"A calm and undisturbed mind and heart are the life and health of the body, but envy, jealousy, and wrath are like rottenness of the bones"* (**Prov. 14:30, AMPC**).

While we should use the keen, intelligent minds God gave us to believe in His healing power, some people use their minds to think themselves into illness. We've all heard of cases where a person entertains such negative, angry thoughts over a long period of time that he or she eventually develops ulcers or even clinical depression or mental illness. Periodically, we hear of someone losing his or her will to live and dying of a broken heart after losing a loved one. The mind and the heart are connected, and God heals both. *"He healeth the broken in heart, and bindeth up their wounds"* (**Ps. 147:3, KJV**).

During His earthly ministry, Jesus healed those who believed He could do so because of who He was. Their faith connected them to His amazing power. Whether God touches us or we reach out and touch Him, real healing takes place by faith. *"Now a woman, having a flow of blood for twelve years, who had spent all her livelihood on physicians and could not be healed by any, came from behind and touched the border of His garment. And immediately her flow of blood stopped"* (**Luke 8:43-44**).

Without a heartfelt belief in the divine power of healing, there are things that all the medicine in the world can't fix. God doesn't want to see us sick. When we agree with Him on this, a marvelous power is unleashed.

> *"And He came down with them and stood on a level place with a crowd of His disciples and a great multitude of people from all Judea and Jerusalem, and from the seacoast of Tyre and Sidon, who came to hear Him and be healed of their diseases, as well as those who were tormented with unclean spirits. And they were healed. And the whole multitude sought to touch Him, for power went out from Him and healed them all."* **Luke 6:17-19**

Although Jesus was God in human form, He was always willing to come down to the level of ordinary people to perform healing. It was true then, and it's true now.

Everything we experience in the natural world originates in the spiritual world, and God's Word brings healing on many different levels. He restores our physical, spiritual, and emotional balance like no one else can. When God touches our minds and spirits, we're healed and made whole again, with nothing missing and nothing broken.

Prayer for Healing

Lord, You are my refuge and fortress. Surely You will deliver me from the snare of the fowler and from the perilous pestilence (**Ps. 91:2-3**).

Man-made Religious Tradition

"God is in control" is a huge statement that really causes many Christians to be less than aggressive with their faith. Seriously, if God is in control of everything that happens on Earth, what's the use of praying for anything or believing for healing? The truth is that God is in control of His ultimate overall plan, but He is not in control of "everything" that happens on Earth.

For example: murder is not God's will–it's directly against the Ten Commandments. Lots of things happen on Earth that are directly against God's will and Word. People sometimes choose sin, wars, murder, stealing, lying, perversions, and even some worship the devil and evil.

On the earth, people have free will to choose to live godly, according to God's instructions, or not. I completely understand that this seems radically different than some religious traditions, but the bottom line is, what does God say about it? I also understand that people never choose to be sick, but sometimes we choose *not* to aggressively resist the works of the devil.

"The heaven, even the heavens, are the LORD's; But the earth He has given to the children of men." **Psalm 115:16**

DIVINE HEALING TRUTH

1. Jesus of Nazareth went about doing good and healing all who were oppressed of the devil. **Acts 10:38**, shows that sickness is Satan's oppression.

2. The Son of God was manifest that He might destroy the works of the devil. Sickness is part of Satan's works. In Jesus's earthly ministry, He always treated sin, sickness, and devils the same. He destroyed them all.

3. A demon was the cause of a boy being deaf and dumb and also the cause of his convulsions. When the demon was cast out, the boy was healed (**Matt 10:1**).

4. Both sin and sickness came into the world through the fall of the human race. The healing for sin and sickness is found in the Savior of the human race.

Lesson 8

Activate God's Power

*Now it happened on a certain day, as He was teaching,
that there were Pharisees and teachers of the law sitting by,
who had come out of every town of Galilee, Judea, and Jerusalem.
And the power of the Lord was present to heal them.*
Luke 5:17

When we're sick, most of us automatically seek out a health care professional. We're so accustomed to following the doctor's orders to speed up the healing process, we don't think about the spiritual side of good health. As previously discussed, there's nothing wrong with physicians and hospitals, but we mustn't lose sight of who is ultimately responsible for healing. When we acknowledge that our Creator wants us healthy and sound, sickness and disease have to go.

Forgetting that healing comes from God is like leaving out the most important link in a genetic sequence. God is not simply a distant supernatural being in another time dimension. He's a personal God who loves us very much and doesn't want to see us suffering or in pain.

"Beloved, I pray that you may prosper in all things and be in health, just as your soul prospers" (**3 John 1:2**). When we experience health issues, we can be quick to blame God and ask Him why He made us sick. This type of wrong thinking is because we simply don't know God's true nature.

He's a good God who wants to give us good things. *"Every good gift and every perfect gift is from above, and comes down from the Father of lights, with whom there is no variation or shadow of turning"* (**James 1:17**). God isn't angry with us, and He isn't intent on punishing us. He's not trying to teach us anything by making us sick. Disease comes from the enemy, not from God.

Battling illness can be frightening and discouraging and put our whole future in question. At times like this, we don't know what will ultimately happen, and we may wonder about our chances for recovery. We have God's Word concerning His plans for us. *"'For I know the plans I have for you,' says the LORD. 'They are plans for good and not for disaster, to give you a future and a hope'"* (**Jer. 29:11, NLT**). Believing this with no trace of doubt gives us hope.

Hope that comes from God brings us joy that can't be extinguished, even with health issues. When we have the kind of joy that He wants for us, it gets down into our hearts and spirits. God is the Great Physician, and even earthly doctors have acknowledged something they may not fully understand yet. Clinging to hope and joy can do more good than medicine and prescriptions alone. *"A merry heart doeth good like a medicine: but a broken spirit drieth the bones"* (**Prov. 17:22**).

Believing in God's ability and willingness to heal is no small thing. Let's take another look at the woman who had suffered from a bleeding issue for twelve years, and no doctor had been able to help her. She touched Jesus's garment and was instantly healed; her healing came not from her actions, but from her faith. *"And He said to her, 'Daughter, your faith has made you well. Go in peace and be healed of your affliction'"* (**Mark 5:34**).

When the doctors give us bad news, we must remember that one of the reasons Jesus went to the cross 2,000 years ago was to make healing available to us right now, when we need it. Medical science continues to look for breakthroughs and cures, but as far as God is concerned, our healing is already done. *"O LORD my God, I cried unto thee, and thou hast healed me"* (**Ps. 30:2**). Agreeing with this activates the missing link.

Speak Healing to Your Body

We all want to see good things happen in our lives, but many of us have no idea how to make those things come to pass. Some people think that the ability to attract anything good to themselves is out of their control and that good fortune randomly descends on only a few chosen individuals. However, luck has nothing to do with it. When we exercise our faith, we can actually bring something into existence merely by speaking the Word.

In the beginning, God brought creation into existence by the power of His spoken Word (**Gen. 1:3-29**). He confidently commanded and literally created something out of nothing. This is awesome, but many people don't realize they have the same power. God the Father gave this power to His Son (**Matt. 28:18**) who, in turn, transferred it to us when we became born again. *"Behold! I have given you authority and power to trample upon serpents and scorpions, and [physical and mental strength and ability] over all the power that the enemy [possesses]; and nothing shall in any way harm you"* (**Luke 10:19, AMPC**).

Believers have the same ability to get results as God. When Jesus walked the earth, He commanded healing and brought the dead back to life. We have been given the same authority. *"…Even God, who quickeneth the dead, and calleth those things which be not as though they were"* (**Rom. 4:17**).

The ability to speak things into existence is actually a spiritual law that comes into play by faith. Jesus demonstrated this power with the centurion who asked Jesus to heal his servant. The man simply asked for verbal confirmation of that healing and believed it before he saw it. The result was supernatural.

> *"And Jesus saith unto him, I will come and heal him. The centurion answered and said, Lord, I am not worthy that thou shouldest come under my roof: but speak the word only, and my servant shall be healed… When Jesus heard it, he marveled, and said to them that followed, Verily I say unto you, I have not found so great faith, no, not in Israel… And Jesus said unto the centurion, Go thy way; and as thou hast*

believed, so be it done unto thee. And his servant was healed in the selfsame hour." **Matthew 8:7-8, 10, 13**

The power of our speech applies to all areas of our lives, whether it's concerning our families, our relationships, our finances, or our jobs. We have the right to command into existence peace in our marriages, happiness in our children, tranquility in our households, and stability in our finances. With this in mind, we must be careful because this works for evil as well as for good. *"A wholesome tongue is a tree of life: but perverseness therein is a breach in the spirit"* (**Prov. 15:4**). Whatever we experience in the physical realm is first born in the spiritual realm.

The tongue can either be a blessing or a curse, and what we repeatedly declare can manifest in us as well as in others. We should be mindful of what we speak into our lives as well as into others' lives. Ignorance of the authority of the spoken word can bring pain and suffering. *"Death and life are in the power of the tongue: and they that love it shall eat the fruit thereof"* (**Prov. 18:21**). It's our choice whether we bring to life something evil or something good; we must speak life.

Prayer for Healing

Lord, You have not given me a spirit of fear. You have given me a spirit of power, love, and a sound mind (**2 Tim. 1:7**).

Man-made Religious Tradition

"Everything happens for a reason." This might be the most common religious tradition. It's repeated by thousands of Christians! This saying insinuates that God has a reason for everything, good or bad. This saying is not based in Scripture and is not true at all! If this was true, why did Jesus say, *"The thief comes to steal, kill, and destroy. But I have come to give you life and that more abundantly"* **(John 10:10)**?

Some things happen because Satan is causing trouble to steal the Word that was sown in your heart. *"Tribulation... persecution... and the cares of this world, deceitfulness of riches, and the lust for other things"* **(Mark 4:17-19)**.

Let the Word Dominate Your Thoughts, Emotions, and Actions

Lesson 9

Take Authority Over All Thoughts

*Casting down arguments and every high thing
that exalts itself against the knowledge of God,
bringing every thought into captivity to the obedience of Christ.*
2 Corinthians 10:5

We live in an imperfect world. Most of us have become accustomed to lack and insufficiency at every level, and simply accepting it as the norm has become the standard way of thinking. This mindset has even extended to our physical and mental health. We tolerate sickness and disease as if it's a part of life; however, illness of any kind is against God's will for us. It should be resisted!

When we realize that God wants us healthy, we'll refuse to tolerate sickness of any kind. *"Beloved, I wish above all things that thou mayest prosper and be in health, even as thy soul prospereth"* (**3 John 1:2**). What He wants for us is wholeness and soundness with nothing missing and nothing broken in our lives. Prosperity in our bodies is good health;

prosperity in our emotions is a sound mind. God wants this for us not just in small amounts, but in great abundance.

Jesus demonstrated this over and over again during His ministry when He healed people wherever He went. God's definition of life far exceeds our expectations. He loves us and wants us to be able to have joyful, abundant lives free of any health issues. *"…I am come that they might have life, and that they might have it more abundantly"* (**John 10:10**). When we have faith in this, He will bless us with abundant health on all levels to the point where the blessings continually overflow.

Jesus actually went to the cross to defeat sickness. *"This fulfilled the word of the Lord through the prophet Isaiah, who said, 'He took our sicknesses and removed our diseases'"* (**Matt. 8:17, NLT**). This type of curse has been permanently taken from us. Despite what we may hear from the doctor or what the medical reports might say, what Jesus did for us carries much more authority. *"Wherefore God also hath highly exalted him and given him a name which is above every name"* (**Phil. 2:9**). Jesus's name is above every other name, including sickness.

Illness has a way of not only draining our physical strength but also weighing down our hearts with depressing, discouraging thoughts. The cure for this is found in the Word of God. *"Anxiety in the heart of man causes depression, but a good word makes it glad"* (**Prov. 12:25**). The "good word" of what God says to us lightens our hearts and gives us back our joy.

No matter how bleak the situation may look, God already made healing available to us 2,000 years ago. He has done His part; we must now do our part and receive it by faith. We demonstrate this faith by exercising biblically based common sense, which we get through constantly studying the Scriptures and putting into practice what we learn. The more we understand about God's Word, the more our spirits are lifted. *"A merry heart doeth good like a medicine: but a broken spirit drieth the bones"* (**Prov. 17:22, KJV**).

There's a definite link between our emotions and our physical bodies, and we can see the results of broken spirits all around us. When we accept what Jesus did and make Him our Lord and Savior, we allow Him to begin putting our broken pieces back together again. The Great Physician has provided physical and emotional healing. It's up to us to agree with Him and accept it for ourselves.

Healed From Within

Life the way God intends for us to live it is a beautiful thing; however, many of us don't have the biblical wisdom we need to enjoy our lives. The result is that we find out the hard way about life's sharp edges and inevitably get hurt. When we're hurting, we can go to God for healing from within.

It's not God's will for us to suffer. When we agree with this, we speed up the healing process. Jesus spent much of His ministry healing people. When He encountered a leper who wondered about Jesus's willingness to heal him, Jesus answered the man emphatically. *"And behold, a leper came and worshiped Him, saying, 'Lord, if You are willing, You can make me clean.' Then Jesus put out His hand and touched him, saying, 'I am willing; be cleansed.' Immediately his leprosy was cleansed"* (**Matt. 8:2-3**).

Too many people wonder if it's really God's will that we receive healing. They may think that something they've done, some mistake or shortcoming on their part, could be hindering it. The leper's doubt can be contrasted with the faith shown by the centurion soldier, who agreed wholeheartedly with Jesus's capacity and willingness to heal, regardless of a person's past.

> *"And when Jesus was entered into Capernaum, there came unto him a centurion, beseeching him, And saying, Lord, my servant lieth at home sick of the palsy, grievously tormented. And Jesus saith unto him, I will come and heal him. The centurion answered and said, Lord, I am not worthy that thou shouldest come under my roof: but speak the word only, and my servant shall be healed… And Jesus said unto the centurion, Go thy way; and as thou hast believed, so be it done unto thee. And his servant was healed in the selfsame hour."* (See **Matthew 8:5-8, 13**)

God is very capable to heal not just physically, but emotionally, as well. The pain from broken relationships is easy to spot when we look at many of those around us. God's Word brings healing and wholeness, and healing begins when we trust Him enough to give our emotional wounds to Him. *"Behold, I will bring it health and healing; I will heal them and reveal to them the abundance of peace and truth"* (**Jer. 33:6**).

When the woman who had suffered with the issue of bleeding for twelve years came to Jesus for healing, she most likely had emotional scars from being rejected and ostracized for so long. However, she believed in Jesus so strongly that she didn't hesitate to go to Him and touch the hem of His robe. Jesus instantly healed her not only physically, but also emotionally. *"And he said to her, 'Daughter, your faith has made you well. Go in peace. Your suffering is over'"* (**Mark 5:34, NLT**).

The kind of healing God offers us comes with peace of mind and the knowledge that good health and wholeness is His will for us. He wants us to enjoy our lives, free from unresolved conflicts and negative emotions that eat us up inside and diminish our quality of life. God is willing and able to put the broken pieces of our lives back together again. When we believe this, we give Him access to our hurts and pains, and enable Him to heal us from the inside out.

Prayer for Healing

Lord, You promised that I will prosper in all things and be in health as my soul prospers. You have blessed me with every spiritual blessing in heavenly places. Lord, You have given me mighty spiritual weapons for pulling down evil strongholds. I make all my thoughts obedient to Christ (**2 Cor. 10:3-5; 3 John 2; Eph. 1:3**).

Lesson 10

God Sent His Word to Heal

He sent His word and healed them,
And delivered them from their destructions.
Psalm 107:20

Most of us would agree that life is better when we're healthy. When we encounter health issues, we have various options on how to deal with them, but not all options will yield the same results. A bad doctor's report can throw some people into a panic. They may even go to God and ask Him if it's His will for them to be healed. His answer to this question is a definite *yes!*

A doctor's number one goal is to restore us to good health, but human expertise always has its limitations. If we get sick, one option we have is to rely solely on the doctor, without bringing God into the mix. This is where things could get dicey.

During Jesus's ministry, the woman who suffered with the bleeding disorder got no results by relying only on human aid but received healing when she went to Jesus.

> *"And a certain woman, which had an issue of blood twelve years, And had suffered many things of many physicians, and had spent all that she had, and was nothing bettered, but rather grew worse, When she had heard of Jesus, came in the press behind, and touched his garment. For she said, If I may touch but his clothes, I shall be whole. And straightway the fountain of her blood was dried up; and she felt in her body that she was healed of that plague."* **Mark 5:25-29**

There's nothing wrong with physicians and medical care, but without faith in God's ability to heal, nothing will happen.

Not only can God heal, but He wants to heal. He's not simply an impersonal God looking down from heaven in a detached manner. When we trust in God for our healing, "if" is never an issue.

We shouldn't make the mistake of thinking that we must somehow "deserve" healing. God heals by His grace, which is undeserved, unearned favor toward us; when we believe this, miracles happen.

God's willingness to heal is independent of our behavior.

The terrible belief that sickness is God's way of punishing us is definitely not God's nature at all. The God who offers us forgiveness for all of our sins is the same God who has made healing available to us. He actually went to the whipping post, and the cross; He bled and died so that we could enjoy perfect health. *"He personally carried our sins in his body on the cross so that we can be dead to sin and live for what is right. By his wounds you are healed"* (**1 Peter 2:24, NLT**). When we have faith in what God did for us, illness doesn't stand a chance.

Healing: Mind, Will, and Emotions

When most people think of healing, they think of it for their bodies; however, the mind is the most significant arena in which healing can take place. Our minds are so powerful that what we think can affect us physically for either good or bad. The mind's ability could be compared to a supercomputer, but infinitely more complex because God created it. When we suffer an emotional wound, the quality of our lives is affected, which is why it's so important to trust the Lord to heal us.

Our minds are more than just physical brains; we are spirit beings living in physical bodies, and we have a soul, which acts as our *thinker* and *chooser*. When we suffer emotionally, how fast we recover or whether we can bounce back at all depends on how we *choose* to respond. Focusing on our pain holds us back from recovering. Meditating on God's Word promotes peace and emotional healing even when we don't understand it.

> *"And the peace of God, which surpasses all understanding, will guard your hearts and minds through Christ Jesus. Finally, brethren, whatever things are true, whatever things are noble, whatever things are just, whatever things are pure, whatever things are lovely, whatever things are of good*

report, if there is any virtue and if there is anything praiseworthy—meditate on these things." **Philippians 4:7-8**

Instead of simply letting negative thoughts hang around, we must consciously examine what we're thinking about. As believers, Jesus has given us authority, so taking authority over our thoughts and choosing to focus on Him is in accordance with spiritual law. The wrong kinds of thoughts cause us turmoil, stress, and misery. Christians are authorized to cast out wrong thoughts and replace them with thoughts that agree with the Word. *"You will keep him in perfect peace, Whose mind is stayed on You, Because he trusts in You"* (**Isa. 26:3**).

We stay trapped in the pain of emotional wounds when we trust in ourselves instead of in God for our healing. This gets us nowhere. We can read self-help books all day long, but we'll make no progress. Relying on Him gives us insight to know what to do when the issue seems so big and insurmountable that we don't know how to deal with it. *"Trust in the Lord with all thine heart; and lean not unto thine own understanding. In all thy ways acknowledge him, and he shall direct thy paths"* (**Prov. 3:5-6**).

Emotional distress drags us down and leaves us feeling hopeless, as if there's no tomorrow. It robs us of our joy and peace. God wants us to know there is a tomorrow, and He is well able to help us move forward. Instead of struggling with it alone, turning over this kind of burden to Him changes our frame of mind. *"Now may the God of hope fill you with all joy and peace in believing, that you may abound in hope by the power of the Holy Spirit"* (**Rom. 15:13**).

The mind can be a dark, sad place, but it can also be a joyful, light-filled place. We don't have to tolerate emotional suffering; that's not God's will for us. *"For I know the thoughts that I think toward you, says the Lord, thoughts of peace and not of evil, to give you a future and a hope"* (**Jer. 29:11**). We can trust Him to lead us out of the darkness into the light. His promises give us healing where we need it the most.

Prayer for Healing

> *Lord, I am redeemed from the curse of sickness. I have the blessings of Abraham, which includes total healing* (**Gal. 3:13; Deut. 28**).

How Confession Helps

A positive-faith confession is agreeing with what God has already said and done. It's declaring who you are, what you have, and what you can do in Christ.

Divine Healing Truth

1. The truth is that healing always comes when we plant God's Word in our hearts. God's will is always healing.

2. God is not using sickness to teach and chastise.

3. God teaches with His Word (**2 Tim. 3:16**).

TO RECEIVE HEALING,
YOU MUST MAKE THE
TRUTH OF HEALING
MORE REAL THAN
THE SYMPTOMS
IN YOUR BODY

Lesson 11

Take Hold of Your Healing

*For assuredly, I say to you, whoever says to this mountain,
'Be removed and be cast into the sea,' and does not doubt in his heart,
but believes that those things he says will be done,
he will have whatever he says.*

Mark 11:23

No matter how long you've been struggling, no matter how serious your situation, healing belongs to you. Even if you feel like you've been standing for so long and you aren't sure if you'll ever see a manifestation, these words are for you. The seed of God's Word, when spoken in faith, works overtime, just like a seed of corn.

Not only are we to expect healing, but we should also believe to live in divine health. John G. Lake said, "Divine health is to live day by day, hour by hour in touch with God so that the life of God flows into the body just as the life of God flows into the mind or flows into the spirit." (*Divine Healing* by John G. Lake.)

Healing is your covenant right. If you want it, it's yours. There's no question about it as far as the Word of God is concerned. The problem is, most Christians haven't truly believed it. They haven't let it reach down into their hearts and become truth to them. God has said it, but they haven't yet believed. If that is the case with you today, know this—it is God's will to heal you. It's in His redemptive plan. It has to be His will because He laid our sickness and disease on Jesus, just as He did our sin (**Isa. 53:5**). God made His Word plain, and He always keeps His Word.

Has an isolated experience caused you to believe maybe it isn't God's will for everyone to be healed? Don't let past experiences be the basis for your belief. Let the truth of God's Word be your standard. God's will for you is healing!

You can take hold of what belongs to you and live in divine health by following the strategies outlined in the Word of God. Here is how you can receive and keep your healing.

1. Take Hold of the Word

> *"Bless the Lord, O my soul, and forget not all His benefits: Who forgives all your iniquities, Who heals all your diseases."*
> **Psalms 103:2-3**

Anytime a believer has a problem receiving or maintaining healing, he or she usually suffers from a lack of knowledge of God's Word and of his or her rights and privileges in Christ. Many people who claim to have faith don't trust God when it comes to healing. They know the promises and they even believe healing is for today, they just don't believe it's necessarily for *them*.

Maybe God won't... That's a dangerous thought.

Here's something you need to understand. Healing *always* comes because Jesus already provided healing and salvation at His sacrifice. If we will plant God's Word in our hearts, then allow the seed to germinate and the plant to *grow* to maturity, we will reap the fruit of a harvest.

God's Word is the vehicle that will get you there. If you are well, God's Word will keep you well. If you are sick, it will heal you and then keep you well. God's Word is medicine, but you must give it attention (**Prov. 4:20-23**). That means you pay attention to what it says, believe it, and act on it.

If you're bogged down and feeling pressure, that's a sure sign you're not giving enough attention to the Word of God. The Word is what causes your life to *work*. It causes healing to come. To stand on the Word of God is to meditate on it and make it the final authority in your life. You put it in your heart until the reality of your healing has more power and validity to you than the symptoms of sickness coming on your body. One thing you must know—*God's Word does not fail!* So, if you catch yourself saying, "Well, the Word isn't working for me," then you know automatically that you are not standing.

Be diligent about keeping God's Word in your heart. Continually read it, listen to it, think about it, talk about it. It will be health to your body (**Prov. 4:22**). And when you get healed, you keep your healing by staying on healing Scriptures and telling people about your healing.

Keep taking the medicine. Keep taking the Word of God. Keep taking that medicine after you're healed and you'll stay healed. The Word of God is life and health.

Say and pray, "I'm bold to take hold!"

2. Don't Consider Circumstances

> *"And being not weak in faith, he considered not his own body."* **Romans 4:19 (KJV)**

To receive healing, you must make the truth of healing more real than the symptoms in your body, but to *keep* healing, the fight is really on. The devil has no intention of letting you keep your healing once you receive it. He's going to try and hoodwink you into giving it up.

So, how do people lose their healing? Satan will send lying symptoms trying to get them to receive it. Then, the minute the first symptoms show up, they say, "I thought the Lord healed me, but I guess He didn't," and when they say that they open the door to the devil. Instead of rising up and meeting the devil with the Word of God and commanding his power to be broken, they yield.

This happened to a man who had been healed in his ears. His hearing had been restored. He was hearing perfectly for several days, but then, about a week later, he couldn't hear anymore. The Lord showed him what happened.

As he went about his daily business, the devil would hop on his shoulder and say, "Did you notice you can't hear as well as you did the other day?" Within a few days, that demon had talked him into losing his hearing. He yielded to it. That's why Jesus said, *"Hold tightly to what you have until I come"* (**Rev. 2:25**).

How do you hold tightly to your healing?

When the enemy comes at you with symptoms of sickness, you can't crawl up in bed and whine, "Why does this always happen to me?" Instead, stomp your foot and say, "Glory be to God! This body is off limits to you, Satan. I refuse to allow you to put that foul thing on my body after Jesus has already taken it for me. So, you might as well pack it up and go home right now!"

It won't always be easy; you have to make an effort. You have to stand for it and fight the good fight of faith, but don't let that scare you. It's a fight you can win. You can win because Jesus gave you everything you need to win. He took your weakness and gave you His strength. He took your sin and gave you His righteousness. He took your sickness and gave you His health. He took every defeat and gave you His victory in its place.

You are the heir of the greatest exchange ever made.

3. Cast Down Unbelief

"And He did not do many miracles there because of their unbelief." **Matthew 13:58 (NASB)**

The only record of anything hindering Jesus from accomplishing the will of God to do mighty miracles occurred in Nazareth. Jesus did heal the people who came to Him, but He could do no mighty works because of their unbelief. Doubt and unbelief will rob you of God's blessings.

The Word of God defeats unbelief. When a person receives the Word, doubt, defeat, and discouragement have to leave. So, don't hang on to any doubt or unbelief. Don't even dwell on it for a moment. Let the Word of God drive it out. Your life depends on it.

Faith should be highly developed in the church concerning healing. If it were, Christians would be as quick to believe they are healed as they are to believe they are saved. But seeds of doubt and unbelief have polluted the hearts of believers.

Remember, doubt comes by hearing unbelief, so be careful what you listen to! God wants you healed, but He works only by faith.

4. Cast Down Worry

"Casting all your care upon Him, for He cares for you."
1 Peter 5:7

There are people right now who are on the verge of a manifestation of healing, and it hasn't come for one reason—they are holding onto their physical condition. In other words, it's all they think about. This is exactly what I was doing before my own wonderful healing testimony.

They worry about whether their medication is working. They think about whether or not they should go back to the doctor, get a different doctor, or try yet another special diet. They are so wrapped up in their condition that they have a tight hold on it and, without knowing it, they haven't let it go and given it to the Lord.

When it comes to receiving and keeping divine healing, Andrew Murray said, "The first thing to learn is to cease to be anxious about the state of your body." (*Abide In Christ* by Andrew Murray.)

God loves you so much. He wants you to give every care, worry, and anxiety to Him. He's the One who can deal with it properly! As long as you are holding onto the care of your sickness, you are taking ownership of it. The Bible says when you do so, you're failing to humble yourself before God (**1 Peter 5:6**).

The Word works. Let the Word fight its own fight. Just rest in God, and one day you'll wake up and your symptoms will be gone.

5. Speak to the Problem

"He will have whatever he says." **Mark 11:23**

Are you speaking to your mountain or letting your mountain tower over you? You see, faith will move mountains, but it won't even move a molehill unless you release it with the words of your mouth. Your prayers should line up with the Word of God—just as the words coming out of your mouth should—to achieve results.

If we are going to obey God, we must talk to the mountain of sickness and cast it out of our lives (**Mark 11:23**). Start speaking the Word today. "Call things that be not as though they were" (**Rom. 4:17 KJV**). As you do, your faith will be strengthened, and your healing will come!

6. Hold Fast Your Confession

"Let us hold fast the profession of our faith without wavering."
Hebrews 10:23 (KJV)

As you put God's prescription for health and healing to work in your life—putting the Word in your heart, speaking it, resisting the devil—don't be discouraged if you don't see immediate results. Sometimes healing comes instantly, but there are other times when it comes more gradually. So, don't let your lingering symptoms cause you to doubt. Cast out every thought the devil sends your way.

Then, having done all to stand, stand until your healing is fully manifested. Hold your ground. Don't waver. **James 1:6-8** tells us that one who wavers and doesn't stand strong is unstable and double-minded and won't receive from God.

Remember this: *"He who promised is reliable and trustworthy and faithful [to His word].... you have need of patient endurance [to bear up under difficult circumstances without compromising], so that when you have carried out the will of God, you may receive and enjoy to the full what is promised"* (**Heb. 10:23, 36 AMP**).

When pain comes, when symptoms come, what do you do? You focus on the Word of God; you focus on the promise. Don't let the devil sway you from your faith stand. Don't move an inch! Hold on tight!

As you put this plan into action–standing on the Word of God, staying out of doubt and worry, resisting the devil, and standing firm–you will position yourself to get and keep your healing. You don't ever have to be sick again. God's best for you is to live in divine health every day. Now, go ahead, receive your healing!

Lesson 12

God's Word is Power-Packed

For the word of God is living and powerful,
and sharper than any two-edged sword,
piercing even to the division of soul and spirit,
and of joints and marrow,
and is a discerner of the thoughts and intents of the heart.
Hebrews 4:12

God's Word is an anointed seed that will grow over time. It's filled with God's power to destroy every yoke of bondage, including sickness and disease!

Some people are always wanting God to speak to them, but if they'd get in God's Word, read it, and meditate on it, they'd find that God is speaking to them from every page. They're always looking for some "new" revelation, yet they haven't mastered walking in the light of what they already know. When you walk in the light of what you know, more light will be given to you. You see, it's the truth of God's anointed Word, not some "new" revelation, that sets people free and destroys every yoke of bondage.

Sometimes when I've tried to read Scriptures to people on healing, they've said, "Oh, I've already heard that." That's like a man sitting down at the table to eat, but when a big T-bone steak is put on his plate, he says, "No, thanks. I've had T-bone steak before." Just because you ate a T-bone steak one time doesn't mean you're never going to eat one again!

> Matthew 4:4
>
> *"Man shall not live by bread alone, but by every word that proceeds from the mouth of God."*

What is this verse saying? It's saying that what natural food is to your body, the Word of God is to your spirit. The Word of God is "food" or nourishment for your spirit. Just because you ate a certain kind of natural food one time doesn't mean you're never going to eat it again. No, you'll come right back to the table and eat the same kinds of food again and again.

> Romans 10:17
>
> *"So then faith cometh by hearing, and hearing the word of God."*

Faith comes by *hearing* and *hearing* the Word of God. In other words, faith doesn't come by hearing it just once, or even by hearing it occasionally. The Word of God is anointed, and if you get that Word in your heart by hearing it again and again, the anointing will set you free.

John 8:32

"And ye shall KNOW the truth, and the truth shall make you free."

The truth sets you free. We know that God's Word is truth (**John 17:17**). The truth of the anointed Word will set you free, but it can't set you free until you *know* it. The way you know the truth is by putting it in your heart–in your spirit. And the way you do that is by hearing the Word continually.

You Must Do Your Part

Healing belongs to us, but most people miss it because they think, *If healing belongs to me, why don't I have it?* In other words, they think the blessings of God are just going to automatically fall on them like ripe cherries fall off a tree, but that's not true. The blessings of God must be *appropriated* by faith in God's written Word. In other words, we must receive by faith the blessings that God has already provided for us in His Word.

The same is true with salvation. For example, have you ever stopped to think about the fact that the new birth, the remission of sin, belongs to the worst sinner just as much as it belongs to the Christian? The remission of sin belongs to people in jail or prison–even those who are on "death row"–just as much as it belongs to the most faithful churchgoer. Why? Because the Bible says, *"For God so loved THE WORLD, that he gave His only begotten Son, that WHOSOEVER believeth in him should not perish, but have everlasting life"* (**John 3:16**).

Jesus paid for salvation for every man, woman, boy, and girl who would ever live on this earth. But people must believe in Jesus and receive Him as their own Savior before salvation can benefit them.

So, salvation belongs to the sinner. Then why don't all sinners get saved? It's either because no one has told them, so they don't know about salvation, or they didn't believe it or accept it.

The same thing is true with healing. One reason many Christians haven't received healing is they haven't heard the Word, and they don't know healing belongs to them. They think they have to stay sick, but healing belongs to them. There are other reasons Christians don't get healed as well, but the point is, healing belongs to them.

We know it's the anointing that destroys every yoke of sickness and disease. Actually, the anointing is released by *acting* on God's anointed Word. That is, by believing it and applying it to your own life.

It's a Done Deal!

God's anointed Word will work for you, too, and set you free from every yoke of bondage—sin, sickness or disease, poverty, or anything else the devil tries to bring against you—but you must *act* on God's Word by agreeing with it. You must believe it and feed upon it. That's how you get it into your heart or spirit.

As God's Word becomes a part of you, the anointing will deliver you and bring freedom to every area of your life. When you believe and act upon God's anointed Word, the anointing will break the yoke of bondage and set you free in every area of your life!

Isaiah 10:27

"... *the yoke shall be destroyed because of the anointing.*"

We often hear it said that it's the anointing that breaks every yoke, but what is a "yoke" in present-day application? A "yoke" is *anything that binds people.* For example, a yoke can be sin, sickness or disease, poverty, or oppression by evil spirits. But thank God, the yoke shall be destroyed because of the anointing!

Testimony of Healing

Kenneth E. Hagin was sickly until seventeen years old. He didn't grow up normally because in his first sixteen years, he couldn't run and play like other children. Kenneth played very limitedly because he had a deformed heart and an incurable blood disease. The blood disease made his blood pale orange instead of red, and there were other complications. He never had a normal childhood and about four months before his sixteenth birthday became totally bedridden.

Several doctors had been called in on his case. The great Mayo Clinic in Rochester, Minnesota, said one of the doctors on his case was one of the best surgeons in the world. This doctor said that no one in Kenneth's condition in the history of medical science had ever lived past the age of sixteen. But thank God for God's Word. *The Word is anointed!* It's filled with God's power, and God's anointed Word destroys every yoke of bondage, including the yoke of sickness and disease. That's how Kenneth was raised up off the bed of sickness–by acting on God's anointed Word.

> **John 16:13**
>
> *"Howbeit when he, the Spirit of truth, is come, he will guide you into ALL TRUTH: for he shall not speak of himself; but whatsoever he shall hear, that shall he speak: and will show you things to come."*

Most of us are looking for something in the natural to help us. But if you are saved, the Holy Spirit abides in your spirit, and God's Word says He'll guide you into all truth. God's Word is truth (**John 17:17**).

"It's All in the Book"

Here's what Kenneth Hagin wrote about his healing:

During the time I was bedfast, the Holy Spirit kept trying to tell me I could be healed. Finally, one day, I heard something on the inside of me – that still, small voice – say, "You don't have to die at this early age. You can be healed." Well, if I could be healed, I wanted to know *how*. I knew medical science couldn't do anything for me. So, I asked the Lord, "*How* can I be healed?" And that same inward voice said, "It's all in the Book."

When I heard the words, "It's all in the Book," I knew the Holy Spirit was talking about the Bible, so I began to diligently study the Bible day and night. When I read Mark 11:23 and 24, those words were branded on my spirit like a branding iron brands cattle. (*Healing Belongs to You* by Kenneth E. Hagin.)

Mark 11:23-24

"For verily I (Jesus) say unto you, that whosoever shall say unto this mountain, Be thou removed, and be thou cast into the sea; and shall not doubt in his heart, but shall believe that those things which he saith shall come to pass; he shall have whatsoever he saith. Therefore I say unto you, What things soever he desire (and that includes healing), when ye pray, believe that ye receive them, and ye shall have them."

Those words, *"…what things soever ye desire, when ye pray, believe that ye receive them, and ye shall have them,"* (verse 24) should become forever imprinted on our hearts.

Isaiah 53:4-5

"Surely he (Jesus) hath borne our griefs, and carried our sorrows (the original Hebrew says He bore our sicknesses, and carried our pains): yet we did

esteem him stricken, smitten of God, and afflicted. But he was wounded for our transgressions, he was bruised during for our iniquities: the chastisement of our peace was upon him; and with his stripes we are healed."

Matthew 8:17

"That it might be fulfilled which was spoken by Esaias (Isaiah) the prophet, saying, Himself (Jesus) took our infirmities, and bare our sicknesses."

1 Peter 2:24

"Who his own self (Jesus) bare our sins in his own body on the tree that we, being dead to sins, should live unto righteousness: by whose stripes ye were healed."

Many times, this is where believers miss it. They say, "I know God promised to heal me, but He hasn't done it *yet*." This causes people to become confused. God didn't promise to heal them *someday*. He said in His Word that they are healed *now!*

To say that God has promised to heal us is like an unsaved person saying, "I know God has promised to save me." No. God didn't *promise* to save the sinner. The Word says that salvation *belongs to every unsaved person right now!* **Second Corinthians 5:19** says, "…*God was in Christ, reconciling the word unto himself, not imputing their trespasses unto them…*" Salvation is a gift. It was paid for by Jesus the Christ. It belongs to us!

Healing belongs to us, too! And receiving healing, just like receiving salvation, is simply a matter of appropriating what already belongs to us because of Christ's redemptive work.

These Scriptures on healing that we just read are not really promises, they are *statements of truth*. In the mind of God, you're already healed. God has already healed you because He laid sickness and disease on Jesus. Jesus has already borne sickness and disease for you. You need not bear what Jesus already bore for you.

When Isaiah wrote about Jesus's redemptive work, *"Surely he hath borne our griefs, and carried our sorrows ..."* (**Isa. 53:4**), he was prophesying about the future. He was looking forward in time to the cross. Some people say that verse was only prophesying concerning salvation; however, the words "griefs" and "sorrows" are literally translated from the Hebrew as "sickness" and "pain." So, our redemption included both remission of sin and physical healing.

When Peter later wrote about Jesus's redemptive work, *"Who his own self bare our sins in his own body on the tree ... by whose stripes ye were healed"* (**1 Peter 2:24**), he was looking back in time to the cross.

Peter wrote, *"...by whose stripes you WERE healed."* Since you were healed, you are healed. In other words, you're not *going to be* healed. You *are* healed! And as you stand in faith on God's Word, your body has to come in line with God's Word, and every symptom has to go!

Someone might say, "I just believe God is going to heal me *sometime*." Well, that's not agreeing with God. In fact, to say that is really taking sides *against* God because God and His Word are one. God's

Word is God speaking to us, and God's Word says we *were* healed **(1 Peter 2:24).**

Lesson 13

God's Healing Power

Because of your unbelief, for assuredly, I say to you,
if you have faith as a mustard seed, you will say to this mountain,
'Move from here to there,' and it will move.
and nothing will be impossible for you.
Matthew 17:20

Do you need healing in your body or your mind?

The "good news" is that healing and health is God's perfect will for you—today! According to God's Word Jesus bore your sins, sickness, disease, pains, and sorrows at the cross (**1 Peter 2:24**.) Believe it! God has given us faith, but sometimes we have too much unbelief.

God's Word Is Like Medicine

God's Holy Word declares that He has sent His Word to heal us and deliver us from our destructions (**Ps. 107:20**). This is an awesome truth that is backed up by God's loving nature. He loves you and wants you to have healing in your body and mind. God created healing for you just like He created and upholds the universe with the word of His power (**Gen. 1:3; Heb. 11:3**)!

God's Word is like medicine and gives healing to all those who will keep His Word fresh in their mind and heart (**Prov. 4:20-22; John 15:7**).

By the Stripes of Jesus

Jesus is God in the flesh. He died on the cross for you and me. Although Jesus walked a perfect life on Earth without sin, the sins and sicknesses of all people were laid upon Him.

The wonderful sacrifice of Jesus was predicted by God hundreds of years in advance. The infallible Word of God declares that we are forgiven by the shed blood of Jesus and healed by the stripes and bruises of Jesus (**Isa. 53:4-5; Ps. 103:1-5**).

There's a Miracle in "Your" Words

The ultimate truth from God's Word is that *"Death and life are in the power of the tongue"* (**Prov. 18:21**). Speak to the problem, cast it out, believe it, and then you'll see it (**Mark 11:23; Prov. 12:18**).

All Things Are Possible

Jesus taught everywhere He went, *"If you can believe, all things are possible to those who believe"* (**Mark 9:23**), and to *"have faith in God"* (**Mark 11:22**).

The Prayer of Faith

God's Word is His will. Don't just ask–always pray by speaking Scriptures. *"Now this is the confidence that we have in Him, that if we ask anything according to His will, He hears us. And if we know He hears us, whatever we ask, we know that we have the petitions that we have asked of Him"* (**1 John 5:14-15**).

Faith is the Victory

God's Word provides many ways to be healed. You can go forward in an anointed prayer service and receive healing through prayer and the gifts of the Spirit (**1 Cor. 12**).

God's Word also provides healing to be received by your own faith.

First John 5:4 guarantees that *"this is the victory that overcomes the world, our faith."* In Mark 5:34, Jesus said, *"Your faith has made you whole."* In **Matthew 9:29**, Jesus said, *"According to your faith let it be to you."*

Prayer for Healing

*Father God in heaven: I pray in Jesus's name according to **1 Peter 2:24**. I believe and receive Jesus as my healer. He bore my sins and sickness at the cross. Now, based on **Mark 11:23**, **Romans 4:17**, **3 John 2**, and **Ezekiel 37:3-9**, I speak to my body, "Be healed in Jesus's mighty name! Muscles, bones, blood, arteries, organs, cells, mind–be healed, in the name of Jesus, Amen!"*

Healing and Wholeness

Good health is an important component of the kind of life God wants for us. When we're healthy and strong both physically and emotionally, we're capable of handling what He wants us to do. The world doesn't know that it's God's will for us to be healed because it doesn't know *Him*; as a result, we see sickness and brokenness all around us. When we're sick, believing His promises about healing allows us to experience it firsthand.

Doctors are limited to what they learned in medical school, but wise physicians admit to miracles they can't take credit for or explain. Psychiatry and modern medicine are still learning about the relationship between the human spirit and the Holy Spirit and the role faith plays in healing.

However, studying the many miraculous healings Jesus performed during His ministry affirms supernatural realities. For those who believe, healing is imminent, despite what it may seem like at the moment. *"To you who fear My name The Sun of Righteousness shall arise With healing in His wings; And you shall go out And grow fat like stall-fed calves"* (**Mal. 4:2**).

Careful analysis of those healings reveals that faith was the common denominator connecting the sick person or a person laying hands on the sick to the power of God.

Restored Physically as well as Emotionally.

Sickness is from the devil, and despite what some religious people say, sickness is not God's will.

When we refuse to accept the world's philosophy and acknowledge the power of the Great Physician, we receive His favor. The Canaanite woman acted on her belief when she asked Jesus to heal her daughter, and He honored her faith. *"Then Jesus answered and said unto her, O woman, great is thy faith: be it unto thee even as thou wilt. And her daughter was made whole from that very hour"* (**Matt. 15:28**).

Now, here's something even more radical—we have that same healing power in us! God gave the power to Jesus who, through His grace and love, passed it on to us. *"Heal the sick, cleanse the lepers, raise the dead, cast out demons. Freely you have received, freely give"* (**Matt. 10:8**).

We're not helpless, and we don't have to tolerate mental illness, depression, physical infirmities, or any other kind of evil tormenting us or our loved ones. Doctors have the best of intentions, but true healing begins in the spiritual realm.

Popular culture shouts at us that sickness inevitably overcomes good health as we get older. However, it doesn't have to be that way.

God only wants good for us. Choosing to have faith and act on what His Word says allows Him to establish His plans for us. *"It will be health to your flesh, And strength to your bones"* (**Prov. 3:8**). Our well-being hinges on what we believe.

God is so good that He has provided several powerful ways for you and me to be healed.

1. By the stripes of Jesus, we are already healed. (**1 Peter 2:24**)

Jesus bore our sicknesses at the same time He bore our sins. It's a done deal in the spirit realm. That's why we need to speak to the problem, (**Mark 11:23**), and pray "Your will be done on earth as it is in heaven. (**Matt. 6:9-10**.)

2. Sowing and Reaping. God's Word is the seed to plant in our hearts. The harvest is the supernatural fruit of healing and blessing! (**Mark 4; Gen. 1**)

3. The gifts of the Spirit (**1 Cor. 12-14**)

4. The believer's authority (**Matt. 16:18-19; Mark 16:17-18; Luke 10:19**)

Let me repeat a suggestion for you to consider. I wish I would have had a better *revelation* of God's Word being the seed to plant in my heart—and getting out the unbelief that the world system promotes—before I had to go through my healing journey!

A "Second Opinion"

Be very *selective* with everything you read and hear. Let me be clear. We all need to be aware of every voice that is obviously anti-Christian, but there are also Christian voices that *"have a form of godliness but deny its power"* (**2 Tim. 3:5**). If you are believing God for healing or a miracle, it is critical that you avoid Christian ministers who teach that miracles and healings have "passed away." This teaching is false and will sow doubt and unbelief in your heart.

Nowhere in the Holy Scriptures does it state that any spiritual gift of power has passed away until we see Jesus face to face (**1 Cor. 13:12**). Doubt and unbelief are the two reasons that faith doesn't receive what God has already provided. We only need a small seed of faith to receive healing (**Matt. 17:20**), as long as we limit our intake of unbelief.

Five Minutes a Day in the Word is not going to Counterbalance Sixteen Hours of Unbelief per Day

Lesson 14

Healing Scriptures to Declare

Our healing will manifest as we believe and declare God's Word as a seed. We need to plant the Word into our heart by believing and speaking. The best way to plant the seed of God's Word in your life is by speaking the Word aloud. Hearing others speak the Word is good but will not produce as bountiful a harvest as speaking the Word yourself.

Speaking God's Word with your mouth is essential. As we speak God's Word, we are planting the seed in our heart for the harvest of results we desire. The problem you face may seem huge. In comparison, speaking God's Word aloud may seem too small. But when planted, that Word will grow in you and overcome the problem.

As discussed earlier, most people expect God's Word to work like a stick of dynamite, but God's Word is like a seed. We know that because of what Jesus said. Jesus said His words are alive. They contain life. The words in God's Word may look lifeless and powerless. Seeds do, too. But they are not without life or power.

In **Mark 4:30-31,** Jesus explained that the kingdom of God works like a seed. So, if we are to understand God's kingdom and how He operates, we need to understand seeds.

Acts 10:38

How God anointed Jesus of Nazareth with the Holy Spirit and with power, who went about doing good and healing all who were oppressed by the devil, for God was with Him.

Matthew 8:16-17

When evening had come, they brought to Him many who were demon-possessed. And He cast out the spirits with a word, and healed all who were sick, that it might be fulfilled which was spoken by Isaiah the prophet, saying: "He Himself took our infirmities And bore our sicknesses."

3 John 2

Beloved, I pray that you may prosper in all things and be in health, just as your soul prospers.

1 Peter 2:24

Who Himself bore our sins in His own body on the tree, that we, having died to sins, might live for righteousness—by whose stripes you were healed.

Proverbs 4:20-23

My son, give attention to my words; Incline your ear to my sayings. Do not let them depart from your eyes; Keep them in the midst of your heart; For they are life to those who find them, And health to all their flesh. Keep your heart with all diligence, for out of it spring the issues of life.

Mark 11:23

For assuredly, I say to you, whoever says to this mountain, 'Be removed and be cast into the sea,' and does not doubt in his heart, but believes that those things he says will be done, he will have whatever he says.

Psalm 107:20

He sent His word and healed them And delivered them from their destructions.

Joshua 1:8

This Book of the Law shall not depart from your mouth, but you shall meditate in it day and night, that you may observe to do according to all that is written in it. For then you will make your way prosperous, and then you will have good success.

Isaiah 53:5

But He was wounded *for our transgressions, He was bruised for our iniquities; The chastisement for our peace was* upon Him, *And by His stripes we are healed.*

Jeremiah 29:11

For I know the thoughts that I think toward you, says the Lord, *thoughts of peace and not of evil, to give you a future and a hope.*

Psalm 115:16

The heaven, even the heavens, *are* the Lord's; *But the earth He has given to the children of men.*

Mark 9:23

Jesus said to him, "If you can believe, all things are possible to him who believes."

Psalm 30:2

O Lord *my God, I cried out to You, And You healed me.*

Matthew 17:20

So Jesus said to them, "Because of your unbelief; for assuredly, I say to you, if you have faith as a mustard seed, you will say to this mountain, 'Move from here to there,' and it will move; and nothing will be impossible for you.

Proverbs 16:24
Pleasant words are like a honeycomb, *Sweetness to the soul and health to the bones.*

Hebrews 4:16
Let us therefore come boldly to the throne of grace, that we may obtain mercy and find grace to help in time of need.

Ephesians 6:10
Finally, my brethren, be strong in the Lord and in the power of His might.

Hebrews 10:23
Let us hold fast the confession of our hope without wavering, for He who promised *is* faithful.

Isaiah 41:10
Fear not, for I am with you; Be not dismayed, for I am your God. I will strengthen you, Yes, I will help you, I will uphold you with My righteous right hand.'

Hebrews 4:14

Seeing then that we have a great High Priest who has passed through the heavens, Jesus the Son of God, let us hold fast our confession.

1 Timothy 6:12

Fight the good fight of faith, lay hold on eternal life, to which you were also called and have confessed the good confession in the presence of many witnesses.

James 4:7

Therefore submit to God. Resist the devil and he will flee from you.

Hebrews 13:8

Jesus Christ is the same yesterday, today, and forever.

Galatians 3:13

Christ has redeemed us from the curse of the law, having become a curse for us (for it is written, "Cursed is everyone who hangs on a tree"),

Psalm 89:34

My covenant I will not break, Nor alter the word that has gone out of My lips.

Philippians 4:13

I can do all things through Christ who strengthens me.

John 10:10

The thief does not come except to steal, and to kill, and to destroy. I have come that they may have life, and that they may have it more abundantly.

Luke 10:19

Behold, I give you the authority to trample on serpents and scorpions, and over all the power of the enemy, and nothing shall by any means hurt you.

Isaiah 55:10-11

For as the rain comes down, and the snow from heaven, And do not return there, But water the earth, And make it bring forth and bud, That it may give **seed** *to the sower And bread to the eater. So shall My word be that goes forth from My mouth; It shall not return to Me void, But it shall accomplish what I please, And it shall prosper in the thing* for which I sent it.

Romans 8:11

But if the Spirit of Him who raised Jesus from the dead dwells in you, He who raised Christ from the dead will also give life to your mortal bodies through His Spirit who dwells in you.

Galatians 6:7

Do not be deceived, God is not mocked; for whatever a man sows, that he will also reap.

2 Peter 1:3

As His divine power has given to us all things that pertain to life and godliness, through the knowledge of Him who called us by glory and virtue.

2 Peter 1:4

By which have been given to us exceedingly great and precious promises, that through these you may be partakers of the divine nature, having escaped the corruption that is in the world through lust.

Romans 10:17

So then faith comes by hearing, and hearing by the word of God.

Matthew 6:33

But seek first the kingdom of God and His righteousness, and all these things shall be added to you.

2 Chronicles 16:9a

For the eyes of the Lord *run to and fro throughout the whole earth, to show Himself strong on behalf of those whose heart is loyal to Him.*

Ephesians 6:16-17

*Above all, taking the shield of faith with which you will be able to quench all the fiery darts of the wicked one. *[17]* And take the helmet of salvation, and the sword of the Spirit, which is the word of God.*

Genesis 8:22

"While the earth remains, Seedtime and harvest, Cold and heat, Winter and summer, And day and night Shall not cease."

Ephesians 3:20

Now to Him who is able to do exceedingly abundantly above all that we ask or think, according to the power that works in us.

Mark 4:26-27

The kingdom of God is as if a man should scatter seed on the ground, and should sleep by night and rise by day, and the seed should sprout and grow, he himself does not know how.

Mark 4:28-29

For the earth yields crops by itself: first the blade, then the head, after that the full grain in the head. But when the grain ripens, immediately he puts in the sickle, because the harvest has come.

Genesis 1:11-12

Then God said, "Let the earth bring forth grass, the herb that yields seed, *and* the fruit tree *that* yields fruit according to its kind, whose seed *is* in itself, on the earth"; and it was so. *And the earth brought forth grass, the herb that* yields seed according to its kind, and the tree *that* yields fruit, whose seed *is* in itself according to its kind. *And God saw that it was* good.

Colossians 2:9-10

For in Him dwells all the fullness of the Godhead bodily; and you are complete in Him, who is the head of all principality and power.

1 John 4:17

Love has been perfected among us in this: that we may have boldness in the day of judgment; because as He is, so are we in this world.

Luke 17:20-21

Now when He was asked by the Pharisees when the kingdom of God would come, He answered them and said, "The kingdom of God does not come with observation; nor will they say, 'See here!' or 'See there!' For indeed, the kingdom of God is within you.

John 8:31-32

Then Jesus said to those Jews who believed Him, "If you abide in My word, you are My disciples indeed. And you shall know the truth, and the truth shall make you free."

John 6:63

It is the Spirit who gives life; the flesh profits nothing. The words that I speak to you are spirit, and they are life.

1 Peter 1:23

Having been born again, not of corruptible seed but incorruptible, through the word of God which lives and abides forever.

Romans 4:20-21

He (Abraham) did not waver at the promise of God through unbelief, but was strengthened in faith, giving glory to God,

²¹ and being fully convinced that what He had promised He was also able to perform.

Luke 17:6

*So the Lord said, "If you have faith as a mustard **seed**, you can say to this mulberry tree, 'Be pulled up by the roots and be planted in the sea,' and it would obey you.*

Romans 12:2

Do not be conformed to this world, but be transformed by the renewing of your mind, that you may prove what is that good and acceptable and perfect will of God.

Healing Is Warfare It's Not a Reward For Being Good

APPENDICES

APPENDICES

Appendix A

Final Words

Are you trying to believe God for healing? Have you been speaking the Scriptures, meditating on them, and planting them in your heart? If you haven't, then you are probably wondering why you aren't seeing any results.

In the natural realm, you cannot grow anything without a seed. It's the same way in the spiritual realm; everything comes from the seed of God's Word planted in your heart.

Please don't take offense. This is vitally important. Wouldn't it be silly for farmers to go out into their field and wonder why they didn't have a harvest of wheat growing in the field when they never planted any seeds?

If you want a harvest, you need to plant some seeds. If you want healing to manifest in your life, you need to take God's promises and sow them into your heart. Take the Word of God that promises you His healing power and meditate on it. Think about, speak it, repeat it, memorize it.

How do you plant the seed of God's Word in your heart? It's not like you just read it one time and that's it. You have to meditate on God's Word until it releases its power, germinates, and begins to release its life (**John 6:63**; **Heb. 4:12**).

To be clear, if you haven't meditated in the Word of God, day and night (**Josh. 1:8**; **Ps. 1:2**), if you aren't studying the Word, and if you don't know or understand what it says, then don't be surprised if you don't get the right results.

> *"Man shall live by every word that proceeds from the mouth of God."* (**Matt. 4:4**)

Five minutes in the Word is not going to counterbalance sixteen hours of unbelief per day. You have to take a healing truth from God's Word and think about it and start letting it control your thoughts, your emotions, and your actions.

Take the challenge to make the study of God's Word a priority in your life. The devil will try to steal the Word from you through trouble and day-to-day busyness that will choke the Word and keep it from producing (**Mark 4:18-19**). In the end, you have the authority to resist the devil and to choose not to become complacent.

If you don't know how to begin planting God's Word seeds in your heart, start with the Scriptures in this book. Look them up in your Bible, meditate on them, and let them take root as revelation knowledge to you personally.

Appendix B

Satan Steals from Us Because of the Way We Think

As a young boy, I experienced God's influence to live a godly life, but I also experienced the sway of Satan with ungodly seed thoughts. One major thought followed me for many years. It was the thought that I would die young. It was a real deception because my own father had died when he was only thirty-four years old.

This is how Satan operates; he brings a thought that seems reasonable and tries to make it grow until you believe it more than you believe in God's blessing and goodness. Satan does the same thing with religious traditions. He brings thoughts and excuses for why it might not be God's will to heal you. It's a lie!

You may not believe everything I say about God's will to heal, but I believe it will be well worth your time to find out what Jesus had to say about healing.

Appendix C
What About Medical Science?

Medical science has made wonderful advances and has saved many lives with amazing results with transplants, surgeries, and early detection procedures to name a few. In fact, medical science is fighting the same enemy that Jesus did with His supernatural power!

Medical science cannot heal the whole world of everything, but the medical community has done some very amazing things! This book will show that God's will is that we fight back against sickness and disease with the power of God, and medical science is fighting the same enemy! The power of God will overcome even impossible circumstances.

Jesus, the Christ, spent three and a half years healing the multitudes, casting out demons, and setting people free from Satan's destroying ways. The Book of Acts shows us that the church continued Jesus's ministry for quite a while, just like Jesus instructed (**Mark 16:17-18**).

However, through the years, the truth of God's will to heal and deliver has been compromised and watered down. Instead of growing stronger in our faith in God and His Word, believers became more and more established in religious traditions. Jesus warned, *"Making the word of God of no effect through your tradition which you have handed down ..."* (**Mark 7:13**).

Another truth that has compromised our faith for healing is that many true believers have not been taught the reality of the born-again experience. Even genuine Christians don't realize the depth of their born-again spirit. They have not known "who they are in Christ." When born-again believers are taught the fullness of what belongs to them because of the "finished work" of Jesus at the cross, death, and resurrection, they begin to resist the devil and his "stealing, killing, and destroying" ways (see **John 10:10**).

Another reason that Christians have not received and fought for healing is the way many Christian leaders have misinterpreted and wrongly taught Scripture.

Appendix D

Guidelines to Use for Interpreting Scripture

1. Always let Scripture interpret Scripture

2. Understand the difference between the Old and New Testaments

3. Never lift a Scripture out of context

4. Interpretation is never based on experience or feelings

5. Never change what God's Word says to match current religious traditions

When we consider the healing power of God, we must consider the supernatural. In other words, we must consider the unseen spirit realm. Many people only consider what they can see in the physical, natural realm, but God's supernatural power must be received with your heart and spirit. This is a whole new way of thinking that many Christians don't know how to tap into!

Let's be real. Most people have a simple religious experience with God. By that, I mean many people experience a gospel message without the miraculous power that Jesus came to demonstrate. Many Christians have adopted this humanistic view of things. What I mean by "humanistic" is that they only look at things on a surface level. They think most everything they encounter on a daily basis is merely physical or natural, but if we rightly divide the truth (**2 Tim. 2:15**) and seek to be spiritually minded (**Rom. 8:6**), we can experience a deeper revelation of the abundant life that Jesus came to give us (**John 10:10b**)!

Prayer for Healing

Father God in heaven: I prayer for every reader to allow the Holy Spirit to lead and guide into all the truth. And that they let the peace of God rule in their hearts in all wisdom. I pray that every reader will let the Word of Christ dwell in their hearts, giving thanks to the Father God for every good and perfect gift from heaven. Be healed, be Filled with the Spirit, be blessed and be a blessing to everyone you meet in the name of Jesus, Amen!

CPSIA information can be obtained
at www.ICGtesting.com
Printed in the USA
BVHW031921190822
645022BV00013B/195